# Opportunity
# SEASON

## How to Launch Your Life Purpose
### A catalyst for every self-help book you own

Kenneth R. Larson

TATE PUBLISHING, LLC

Knowledge is Power;
Knowledge plus doing is Success;
Opportunity Season helps you
"do" your Knowledge.

## Participants talk about Opportunity Season:

"The weather, sports and life come and go in seasons, so it is natural to embark upon life enhancing partnerships, dialog, spiritual growth and greater action toward taking advantage of your opportunities in twelve-week cycles. I have read dozens of self-help, spiritual and motivational books. Ken has written a great book that goes beyond theory and gives you an actual road map for success. Just like sports, life achievements are more attainable with a team, a coach and partners to help you with encouragement, perspective and accountability. *Opportunity Season* outlines not just how to create this structure but how to implement it every day."

Scott Whitehouse
Former Running Back EFL
(European Football League)
Marketing Executive

"*Opportunity Season* has been an invaluable experience for me. Being focused has always been one of my strong suits, but working with a partner, as well as a spiritual group, has brought a new awareness to my life. For me, the unique thing about our season was not achieving goals, but rather about me being mentored spiritually as I was accomplishing my goals. The Weekly Game Plans were very uplifting. The process of mentoring seems to be a lost art. This has been a great experience for me."

Bill Wilkey
Business Entrepreneur

"I have read *Opportunity Season* and more importantly I have recently incorporated it into my life. It is a book that will lead one to the accomplishment of one's dreams. It is a "how to" book that can take the encouragement of John Eldredge, Rick Warren and others to fruition. It is a system that can motivate behavior via a team concept and team accountability."

Scott McClaine
Real Estate Developer

"*Opportunity Season*? I thought, 'This is just another accountability process,' and then after listening to the changes in Ken's own life and others, I thought I'd better slow down and get some clarity on exactly how this was or was not different from other 'accountability' groups I'd been a part of in the past. What a refreshing surprise this book was! It defies the stereotypical label of either self-help or motivational, because it does both but is more than either of those labels. Most self-help books leave you over-diagnosed and under-prescribed with practical tools to cure what ails you. That is not the case with Opportunity Season. It is a profoundly simple (yet not over-simplified) vehicle that will walk you through to practical, lasting breakthroughs because the concepts are anchored in knowing the truth. Ken has a way of addressing difficult subjects quite simply without drowning people in detail. Having served in the capacity of Biblical Counselor for several years, I can heartily endorse the need for this book. It fills a unique role that blends truth-based self-realization with active behavioral change that is not an easy blend for most people. Congratulations on a job well done."

Deborah Wittmier
International Bible Teacher

"Ken has provided a valuable tool for Christians who are looking to leverage biblical teamwork and account-ability in order to pursue and achieve their over-arching goals. *Opportunity Season* is sure to put practical feet to those frustrated by limited production and inactivity."

Sean Dunn
Champion Ministries

"Participating in an *Opportunity Season* has been a life-changing event. It is one thing to try and describe it, and quite another to experience it. *Opportunity Season* is so much more than a self-help plan or an accountability group. The materials, general guidelines, and team con-cept will help you to prioritize the important areas of your life. This is a must-read book and a must-"do" season for anyone who wants to keep growing and learning."

Robert C. Silva
Developer

"The first thing that excited me about Opportu-nity Season was the chance to commit for 12 weeks and to be able to measure winning and losing on a week-to-week basis. This is the 1st men's group that tapped into my sense of competitiveness! This was a great format for me to make significant and measured changes in multi-ple areas of need in my life. The 1st season had such a great impact on me that I gladly signed up to be a group leader for my next season. Seeing the change that can be accomplished in men's lives through this simple and specific format was a great motivator to take the next step in leadership. Little did I know that I would experience even more personal growth through leading other men through Opportunity Season as well!"

Blake Frye
CEO-Interstate Connections of Colorado, LLC
President-Pinnacle Forum Colorado

"The open-ended, flexible structure is very appealing in a wide variety of settings."

Judy Berdal
Reading Instructor

"*Opportunity Season* is a true blessing. This book gives people a way to work as a team, as a partner, one-on-one, and as an individual, on opportunities in their lives while inviting the Lord to be a part of it. It is also likely that one *Opportunity Season* will not be enough."

Steve Lencke

"Participating in a couples *Opportunity Season* worked great. Husbands were teammates, wives were teammates and both couples together made the team. The format allowed for interaction with your teammate as well as your spouse."

Ellen Schmitz
Homemaker

"*Opportunity Season* is a companion volume and catalyst for every self-help book you have ever read."

Mike Hamel
Author, *The Entrepreneur's Creed*

"*Opportunity Season* was a great experience. The fruit of the exercise is a deeper relationship with another believer–those 10-minute daily talks and prayer will return much greater dividends in future friendships. *Opportunity Season* not only provides concise reading material, but also some practical exercises, scripture memory and 'homework' that help stimulate the relational connections. Don't take *Opportunity Season* lightly–if you put the effort in you will definitely reap the rewards."

Shannon L. Dreyfuss
CHCC

**Opportunity Season**
**How to Launch Your Life Purpose**
A catalyst for every self-help book you own
By Kenneth R. Larson

"Opportunity Season" by Kenneth R. Larson

Unless otherwise noted, Scripture quotations are taken from the *Holy Bible, New International Version* ®, Copyright © 1973, 1978, 1984 by International Bible Society. Used by permission of Zondervan Publishing House. All rights reserved.

Scripture quotations marked "KJV" are taken from the *Holy Bible, King James Version*, Cambridge, 1769.

Scripture quotations marked "NKJV" are taken from *The New King James Version* / Thomas Nelson Publishers, Nashville: Thomas Nelson Publishers. Copyright © 1982. Used by permission. All rights reserved.

This book is designed to provide accurate and authoritative information with regard to the subject matter covered. This information is given with the understanding that neither the author nor Tate Publishing, LLC is engaged in rendering legal, professional advice. Since the details of your situation are fact dependent, you should additionally seek the services of a competent professional.

ISBN: 1-5988636-6-5

060706

# Dedication

**To: Carl A. Larson,**

My father,

Bronze Star recipient,

Lay-Minister,

Small Business Owner

Who in the Philippines, in World War II, while in a fox hole, in the rain, with bombs going off, *decided*:

## Happiness was a Choice

# Acknowledgments

Thank you to Donald R. Vance Ph.D., Associate Professor of Biblical Languages and Literature at Oral Roberts University for his review of the material and checking of the Biblical references. Thank you Don, also, for being my teammate in one of my early seasons.

Thank you to my many team members and teammates for encouraging me and letting me "try out" the concepts on you. Without your belief in me and willingness to try something different, *Opportunity Season* would not exist.

Thank you to my wife, Mary. When asked recently to give a one-word description of my wife of 31 years, I replied support. You have been with me through the years and have supported most of my "crazy ideas." I love you.

Thank you to the Prayer Summit group who have prayed for and encouraged me year after year.

Thank you to Joe Thackwell for editing.

Thank you to Jeff Slemons for the great illustrations. www.slemonsillustration.com

# Opportunity Season
# Table of Contents

# Foreword

There are thousands of self-help books available today, many of which have useful material. Yet most people never follow through on the wisdom contained therein. The problem isn't with the information but with the implementation. *Opportunity Season* features a unique *Results Operating System* that makes it easier for people to turn content into life-change. It functions like the operating system in a computer by providing a framework on which various software programs can run.

The beauty of *Opportunity Season* is that it doesn't compete with other self-help books; it compliments them, making it a valuable addition to any personal growth library.

*Opportunity Season* is based on biblical wisdom and is structured in a 12-week program that capitalizes on the strengths of teamwork and peer coaching.

A search for "personal growth" books on Amazon returns over 10,600 titles. Type in "self-help" and get 32,000 listings. *Opportunity Season* is a unique companion volume to these books. It's an easy-to-follow approach to putting into practice what they suggest.

A more spiritual name for the process described in *OS* is peer discipleship.

Mike Hamel
Co-Author of *Giving Back: Using Your Influence to Create Social Change*

# Introduction

# Why Trying Isn't Good Enough

A few months ago a group of men and I were having dinner with a successful Christian leader. He is a self-made, multi-millionaire from his former business career. He has a great family and a fantastic wife. He is older and is starting to feel that he has successfully run the race that was set before him. We asked him what he was currently excited about, and a passionate reply ensued concerning a recent seminar that he had attended, where the speaker had suggested that those in attendance implement a new type of goal setting for the coming year.

Those of us at dinner became excited about the idea as well when he shared the information with us. Sensing our interest, this Christian leader suggested that those of us gathered with him implement the idea in our lives. In response, one of our group asked if he had instituted the practice in his life. His answer, "Of course not, but I would like to. Maybe I will try it next year." I believe he really meant what he said and wanted to implement this practice into his goal setting the following year. Unfortunately, for him and those of us gathered with him, the only thing that is likely to happen is that we will all acquire another *try* in our lives. Another great idea to be filed away in our brains, never to be heard from again.

Instead of being able to make a decision concerning this information, it was relegated to the ***things I would like to try file***. Most successful people have a very large ***want*** *to try file*. What if there was a way to handle this decision differently? What if you could actually make a decision about the idea presented. It might look something like this: after asking yourself, "Do I choose to implement this into my life?" your "Yes" or "No" comes with a confidence that this internal answer is the correct one. What I'm talking about is our ability to choose the ideas we would like to implement in our lives, or not, depending on their ability to move forward our life purpose and goals.

I am guessing that you are probably like me. I am guessing this because you picked up this book and you bought it. If you are like me, you have picked up many books like this. Many of them claim to be the last book you will need about growth, success, or the most fantastic life that you could imagine. When you finish reading these books, many times you are convinced the ideas will change your life for the better. You have probably said with me, "If I could just implement the strategies in this book, **then** I would be successful. I would be healthy, wealthy, and wise. I could complete my quest. I would be fulfilled. I would be a whole person. I would have the things that I want in my life."

The same thing has happened to me when going to seminars. At the end of the seminar, I am really excited. Usually these seminars conclude on Saturday afternoon, and I will be flying home on Sunday. My head is full of ideas I want to implement on Monday, to start the process of *changing my life*. But, on Monday, when I arrive at work there is a stack of undone things, unanswered e-mail, voice mails, and my assistant asking me to complete tasks that were undone while I was gone. This was to be *the time* when I was *really* going to change things in my life, to make this the first day of my spectacular life.

In an earlier time in my life, when I was in my early twenties, I would be talking to my dad on a week-end home and say, "I've really found it this time. This is *the* answer. This is the thing I've been looking for." He would smile, and he would say, "Well, that's really good." But, he never seemed to get as excited as I was. He never seemed to want to implement this new bit of incredible wisdom into his own life. Even though I knew he was truly happy for me and desired my success, I would think, "He just doesn't get it, he just does not understand the valuable information that I have discovered. If people only knew this new information I had come to possess this would be a different world."

I am older now (I'm almost fifty) and I am starting to understand a little bit of the wisdom that my dad was showing. It was not that he did not have passion for life, and that he did not want to move forward. It was because he had already heard the "new" information I was present-ing to him. He knew from experience that there really are not many new things *under the sun*.

We have been presented with, and therefore know, many of the things that are needed for us to become wildly successful. We are full of the knowledge of success. What we lack many times is the execution of the things we need to do. I have come to believe that *the* thing that holds us back is not the lack of information, or failure to think our way into a "better me" in ninety days or in five easy lessons; instead, we lack a strategy for implementing the information we already possess. We possess the infor-mation we need; and, many times, it is the exact informa-tion we need. Therefore, it is the lack of execution and application of the information to our lives that keeps us from success, creating the areas we would like to change in our lives. In the end, this change will only happen with results; for new ideas or new concepts will not have a great impact on our lives unless the ideas are implemented in our lives and the results show up in our lives.

I would like to explore this with you further to help you gain an understanding of some of the problems we encounter when we are trying to accomplish the goals we have for our lives. I congratulate you for having the desire and the mind set to try to discover how you can reach your goals. You probably have improved yourself considerably by having an open attitude towards learning, and trying to move forward.

Let us start by exploring this idea of try. T-R-Y, what is try? I think I will *try* to get in shape. I think I will *try* to write a book. I think I will *try* to be the best salesman in my company. I think I will *try* to have a good marriage. I will *try* it, and see if I like it. All this trying is what we do on New Year's Day. We are going to *try* to be better. We really mean it. But the hard, cold facts are that we are not rewarded for trying in society. We are rewarded for results.

Schools trained us that if we try, we can be rewarded. We were given B's and C's in school for just trying. It sometimes did not matter if we learned the material but only if we tried. I am not opposed to this thinking in a learning environment. I actually think *try* is a big part of learning. But *society* does not reward us for trying. It only rewards us for results. It rewards us for the things we do. Not for the things we know, not for the knowledge we have, and not for the things we try. It only rewards us for the results we demonstrate in life; be they mental, physical, or spiritual. Therefore, trying is only important if we find out what works and what does not work. If something works, we should continue doing it and do more of it. If something does not work, we need to quit doing it. The only reason for trying something is to make a decision. Do I want to continue to do this, or do I want to quit doing this?

I've noticed that there is an interesting and subtle

thing about trying that makes us feel good. I do not know why. Maybe it is because we have been conditioned by school to think that trying is a good result. We seem to be conditioned to chatter about all the things we are trying to accomplish, even if it is only for show.

"Ken, what are you doing with yourself these days?"

"Well, I'm trying to get my weight down. I'm trying to get my sales up. I'm trying to work on my marriage."

"Oh, that's really good, what are you doing?"

"Well, I'm trying to get a workout program going. I went to the fitness center, and I bought a membership, so I can try to get in shape."

No commitment to results is made by trying. There is plenty of trying. Trying somehow seems better than not trying because we are at least doing something. However, is trying really better if we do not execute and get results? Especially when we keep trying the same solution with the same poor result. We should keep in mind that a popular definition of insanity is expecting different results by trying the same thing. This book is about results.

If we do get motivated to change something about our lives, we usually go back to *trying* the same things we have tried before, rather than coming to the conclusion that the goal was right, but the things we were trying in the past did not produce results. Even if the previous solution did not work when we tried it before, we seem to gravitate back to the same solution. Maybe we need to *do* something different. Not try something different, but do something different. And, if it does not work, we need to do something different again. Not just operate in "try." Seems too simple doesn't it. If a strategy does not work, I need to recognize that and keep doing something different until the desired result shows up in my life.

There is another aspect of *try* that involves the *stuff* we have. We speculate, "If I had the right stuff . . . if I had the right information . . . if I had the right luck . . . if I had the right job . . . if I had a wife that supported me . . . if I could find the right church . . . if I could find friends to support me . . . then something good would happen in my life. I would be successful." This is just an elaborate excuse. It can make us feel good; but only because we think we are trying to find the correct solution.

Many times, we blame education. We plead our case, saying, "If I had the correct education, then I would be able to do . . . whatever it is." However, what we should do is to simply make an informed decision to obtain the education, or not. If you get the education, you have eliminated the excuse. If you decide not to get the education you still will not have lack of education as an excuse any more. The decision is not, "If I had this, then. . . ." The decision is, "Should I get this information through education or not?" More importantly, "Am I willing to pay the price to get the education that I need to do the things that I desire to do?" Yes or no. End of trying and start of results.

When I started my profession as a stockbroker, I started with a company that was not considered a "name brand" firm in the city I was in. By that I mean the company was not well known. When I called investors and gave the name of the company where I worked, the person I was calling would not recognize the name of the firm, even though we were members of the New York Sock Exchange. I am sure that when you think of stockbrokers, there are only two or three companies that come to mind. I kept using this as an excuse as to why I was not executing or fulfilling my dream of becoming a stockbroker. What I eventually did, was to change firms. I joined a firm that had a "brand name." One of my main reasons in doing that, which made all the difference in the world, was to eliminate one of my excuses for not being able to execute my dream. As long as I said, "Well, the reason I'm not successful is the lack of name recognition of my firm . . ." and accepted this reason for failure, I could not be successful.

Therefore, when I admitted to myself that I had two choices, I could either change the firm I worked for, or eliminate that belief. I needed to make a decision and overcome the excuse. The choice I made was to go to a new firm. Eventually, I learned that it was me that needed to change, not the name on my business card. So, by the end of the story, the real good news is that by eliminating one of those *tries*, I was able to understand and learn what the real problem was. The real problem was not the name on my business card, but my execution of my business plan. Thus, one of the very important things about *trying* is that trying can help you identify and eliminate things that are not working in your life, so that you can start executing things that do work in your life.

To explore the positive aspects of trying, I would like to also introduce you to one of my favorite words: *chimera*. A chimera is fire-breathing monster in Greek mythology. It has a lion's head, a goat's body, and a serpent's tail. In essence, a chimera is an imaginary monster composed of incongruous parts; and therefore, the word has come to describe an illusion or fabrication of the mind, especially an unrealizable dream or a fantasy. Thus, I conceive of chimeras as the monsters that hold us back through our fear of failure or fear of success. While I do not aim to explain all aspects of those fears (there are plenty of good books on the subject), I am captured by the notion of chimeras as the monsters of "I can't do" or "I would try it, but. . . ." These monsters are only in our head.

They can not be real, because these monsters are made up of parts that cannot possibly be put together. By definition a chimera is a myth. We can hold on to our myth for many years because we and other people are willing to accept the excuse that our problem is this fire-breathing monster. The truth is the monster is only in our mind; made up by us to make us feel better.

To move forward, we may need to deal with our chimeras. Chimeras are those funny things that we build up in our mind. They are not real. They are made of things that can not be, of serpents and lions and different body parts that are put together. Even though these imaginations are not real, they appear to be so real that they hold us back. Unfortunately, we prefer to look at the world through our chimeras rather than the light of objective truth. These are the imaginations that Paul talks about in II Corinthians 10:5, "Casting down imaginations, and every high thing that exalteth itself against the knowledge of God, and ***bringing into captivity every thought to the obedience of Christ.***" (KJV) As strange as it may seem many times we would rather believe imaginations rather than the truth of the Bible or the truth of hard facts.

These imaginary chimeras are mists or veils that can hold us back from looking for the truth. We need to be willing to bring them into the light. If we would be willing to *take them out and look at them*, or talk about them with someone else, we would discover that we are holding on to them because we do not want to pay the price of success. Instead of having real success, or having the real results show up in our lives, we can tell ourselves or con ourselves into believing that we really would have the success we desire, except for this chimera. Our deception goes like this, "If I did not have this imaginary monster in my way;" which may be education, knowing the right people, being born on the right side of the tracks, or whatever it is in each individual's mind; "then I could be successful."

"And Oh, by the way, if I wanted to be a successful person, I could be; that is, if I chose to be. I just choose not to be, because of my chimera." These thoughts, in some *crazy* way, make us feel in charge of our lives. We foolishly think that it really is this imaginary monster that is holding us back. It even allows me to think that I have made the choice not to be successful. For example, we can rationalize our lack of success by claiming that really successful people have to "step on people" to get to the top. Successful people need to be "a little dishonest" to get to the top. Successful people do things that I am not willing to do because I am more holy and have more common sense. This sounds reasonable, for we can easily reference examples of such people; however, this is simply the power of the illusion; for, often, the underlying truth about this excuse-giver is that he or she will not go to the cutting edge and do the things that are necessary for success. Truly successful people know who they are (including what they will and will not do), where they are going, and are seeing results show up in their lives.

We build this big monster, this big chimera, and let it live between who we are and who we could be. You have the ability to be just as successful as the people who are on the other side of that veil; who are on the other side of that monster and living their dreams in the "*castle*" protected by that monster. There is a chance that you truly do understand the correct reasons you are not living at the level you desire. If you do, that is great. For the rest of us, we usually need others to help us identify our chimeras.

The Israelites decided to not follow God into the Promised Land because of a chimera. The chimera they encountered was their perception of the "giants" in the land. They were so taken by this chimera that they felt like grasshoppers. Because of this lack of faith in God and his destiny for their lives, these particular Israelites spent the rest of their lives wandering in the desert and never fulfilled God's destiny for them, his chosen people.

When we are willing to choose wisely and start using the information we have acquired about our real problems, the possibility of living the life God called us to becomes a real possibility. God believes in us to a far greater degree than we believe in ourselves. He has chosen us and has wonderful plans for our lives. That does not necessarily mean money, power, prestige; it might, but what I am talking about are the things that God has put in my heart–the life that I desire in my heart because it is my destiny, my God-given vision. When we understand the beautiful reality of this vision, we must ask why we are willing to believe in an imaginary monster–the mental chimera that stands between us and the living out of our God-given destiny.

This brings us back to *try*. The path to success that you may be on has steps. As we have seen, most of us start by trying things. Then, if we do not achieve the success we have in our hearts by trying, we start to make excuses. When we are older, we may sort through some of the "tries" we have had. We may quit trying, but the desires of our heart are still there. So, we get more sophisticated. We put chimeras in front of us to make sophisticated excuses as to why we have not achieved our dreams. Some people call these sophisticated excuses "plateaus," but we are calling them chimeras because of the visual imagery of a self made monster that stops us in our minds from walking into the life of our calling.

What is your favorite excuse for not living or being

or having the things you really want in your life or your destiny? More importantly, what excuses keep you from the things that God has called you to be? While these are important questions, we will start, not by worrying about what excuses we have, but by deciding what the "castle" looks like. This is a very important first step. We want to explore what God has put in your heart. You have probably done this exercise sometime when trying to define your passion, or understand your vision, or your call, or the thing that defines you.

In the movie "City Slickers," when Curly is talking to Billy Crystal, he says, "You must find the one thing that defines you, and focuses you, and gives you meaning, to get you beyond the burn out you feel." As the movie portrays, this kind of passion is a very powerful force. Therefore, we will take our own journey towards that "one thing," towards the "castle" we would like to live in, the desires of our heart. The next step becomes logical: get through the chimeras that are holding us back from that calling. If we do this, we succeed in not allowing excuses to rob us—in not allowing the tyranny of trying to rob us from our rewards.

An Opportunity Season, as described in the next couple of chapters, will give you a tool. A tool that gives you leverage. A tool that gives you the ability to accomplish something that you could not accomplish before without the tool. I call this tool "Opportunity Season," and it is a result of what I have learned, alongside others, that has enabled us to break through our chimeras. However, I do not claim that this is the last self-help book you will ever need. That is not the idea of *Opportunity Season*. You are actually going to need a number of books, as they contribute to the necessity of quality information. The huge difference is that you are going to start executing the great ideas you learn rather than just reading about them.

Instead of trying to think your way into success, you are going to start acting and doing your way into success. If you learn something new and want it worked into to your life, add it to your next Opportunity Season. It is just that simple and just that hard.

I believe that, for the majority of people who have picked up this book, it is not a lack of information that has caused you to miss your dreams. You may truly believe that knowledge is power. To a certain extent, I agree. However, what I have found in my life is that knowledge is not necessarily power. Knowledge might just be good conversation. Knowledge might help me identify my chimeras. Knowledge may define, in a very eloquent way, why I am not living in the "castle of my dreams"—why I am not executing the vision and plan that God has for my life.

In the next couple of chapters, I want to give you some strategies for accomplishing some of the things on your journey. However, you are not going to take this journey alone. This is key. According to the powerful Biblical principle of community, I am recommending that you gather together people around you for this journey. Central to this community is a teammate who is a peer and fellow traveler; someone who will partner with you in the mutual achievement of each other's opportunities or goals. An added level of community is comprised of four to six additional participants who make up our team.

The next two chapters will describe an Opportunity Season to you. It will give you a tool that will give you the added leverage to move you toward your opportunities and goals. This tool will move you from having knowledge to doing knowledge. This is where the power is. It is not that knowledge is power, but that execution of knowledge and correct thinking moves you toward your legacy and its goals. In other words, this tool accelerates and turbo-charges your efforts to follow your call.

Back to the Christian businessman leader we started with. If he really wanted to work this discipline into his life he could do that with Opportunity Season. How many ideas have come your way that you wanted to work into your life? Too many. My response to you (and myself) is that if you want to work something into your life, just put it in your next season and watch it show up in your life as results, not just another good idea that you wish you were doing. You will also remove all the stress of the things you *should be doing* and start progressing toward and doing the things you want to do to further your calling.

What I really desire for you is that you will implement the concepts in this book. My hope is that you start having your own Opportunity Season. If you just read this book and learn some new information, I will have failed you. If you use the tool of Opportunity Season to start *doing* some of the great information locked in your brain, you will be the winner and I will have succeeded in my goal. You may be thinking of a goal right now that you have tried to work into your life. Opportunity Season is quite possibly the tool that will equip you to accomplish the results you desire to see in your life.

# Try

**2 Corinthians 10**

⁵Castingdownimaginations,andeveryhighthingthat exalteth itself against the knowledge of God, and *bringing into captivity every thought to the obedience of Christ;*(KJV)

**Numbers 13**

³² And they spread among the Israelites a bad report about the land they had explored. They said, "The land we explored devours those living in it. All the people we saw there are of great size. ³³ We saw the Nephilim there (the descendants of Anak come from the Nephilim). *We seemed like grasshoppers in our own eyes, and we looked the same to them.*"

**Psalm 37**

³ Trust in the LORD and do good; dwell in the land and enjoy safe pasture. ⁴ Delight yourself in the LORD and *he will give you the desires of your heart.* ⁵ Commit your way to the LORD; trust in him and he will do this:

An Opportunity Season combines the Biblical principles of Fellowship, Accountability, Discipleship, and Asking God to turn your knowledge into results.

# Chapter 1
# What's an Opportunity Season?

We all want to be successful. We may not even know how to define success, but we know we want to be successful. You want to be a successful person or you would not have picked up this book. You might feel that you are already successful and you want to be more successful; but, unfortunately, the bottom line is that very few of us achieve our full potential. Thus, there are many types of help available. Mentoring, coaching, training, self-help books, and even luck may have played or will play a role in your success. Then, there are some of you who are successful because you just intuitively *do things right.*

The Bell Curve, which you might remember from your high school days when the teacher *graded on the curve*, looks at the percentages of people who fall into the categories of average, good, or excellent.

About 60 percent of the people fall into the category of average. None of us think we are average, but about 60 percent of us are. If you go further out on the curve, about 15 percent naturally break into the above average or below average category. About 1 to 3 percent are exceptional—either exceptionally good or exceptionally bad. Our focus for now is on the exceptionally good or talented in whatever category we are interested in. Obviously where you may fit on the bell curve has to do with the data set being observed. Professional athletes would be in the upper category for their sport, but may fall in the bottom when it comes to relational skills at home. I am not trying to pick on professional athletes; but, I read the paper, and some exceptional athletes are bad actors in their home life even though they are pros on the field of play.

The interesting thing is that intuitively there are 1 to 3 percent of people who are just innately or intuitively successful. Maybe that is how God made them, or maybe that is just luck (which I do not really believe in); but, for some reason, about 1 to 3 percent of the population is successful in any given area.

For the rest of us, we need a tool or something to give us leverage to help us obtain our desires. I believe that Opportunity Season is the tool that can provide the leverage to allow us to get through the chimeras talked about in the introduction. Opportunity Season can provide us the leverage to get through the things that are holding us back. Therefore, Opportunity Season is designed as a tool that provides a methodology for producing the opportunities or goals we want to show up in our lives. I have found if I want something to show up in my life, it is as simple and hard as adding it to my next Opportunity Season.

The structure of Opportunity Season is very simple. An Opportunity Season is twelve weeks, much the same as a sports season, a business quarter, or the seasons of the year. The participants in the season are your teammate (one other person) and a team of teammate pairs. Most of the contact between participants is by telephone. Daily calls are 10 minutes in length between teammates. Weekly Team calls, again usually on the telephone, are made between all participants. Chapter Three will give you a full description of an Opportunity Season. A jargon sheet is also included at the end of Chapter Three to help you remember the structure. Opportunity Season is simply a *tool* that will allow you to achieve accelerated growth in areas of your life that are important to you. You decide what is important and use Opportunity Season to accelerate your progress toward your opportunities or goals.

Tools are critical when building things or changing things. If you have ever worked in construction, you know how exquisite it is to have the correct tool to complete the job before you. If your goal is to have a hole, you need a power drill. You also want a very sharp drill bit. The drill with the sharp bit easily helps you obtain the hole you need. You know what you need, a hole. Thus, the drill becomes an extension of your hand that gives you extra leverage to accomplish the goal with ease.

In ancient times (Stone Age times), if a caveman wanted a hole, he knew that to get a hole he needed a harder material to abrasively rub on a softer material to get that hole. There was not much power, strength or leverage in that system, but a caveman was able to produce the hole he needed using this system. We can apply this same concept to our lives when trying to reach our goals. We look for tools or technologies or knowledge to apply to our life to provide leverage to obtain the things we want. If we can find the correct tool or the correct knowledge or the correct technology, we can achieve our goals with less effort.

People say that knowledge is power. To a certain degree, knowledge is power, but I think knowledge is only powerful with execution. We need knowledge to determine what is needed to be successful. In terms of the hole illustration, we need the knowledge that a hole is what we need. However, like the ancient man who was aware of both his need for a hole and the basic principle behind making a hole, we can find ourselves without the tools to easily execute our goals. While books and seminars can provide us with endless knowledge, many times we only receive knowledge. What is needed is a tool to compliment this knowledge and equip us to break through our chimeras by putting ideas into practice. Thinking in terms of percentages, it could be that our progress toward a given goal is 20% related to effective knowledge and 80% related to the execution of that knowledge. For some reason we tend to think of it the other way around, 80% knowledge and 20% execution.

This problem has been with mankind for many years. In Hebrews, chapters 11 and 12, the author addresses this problem He states in Hebrews 12:1 that we are surrounded by a great crowd of witnesses. This great crowd of witnesses is described in chapter 11 as consisting of people who were successful in the faith. They overcame the odds through the power of God and through the *application* of their faith, achieving their God-given destiny. One of the things they needed to do was to throw off everything that hinders them–the things that weighted them down. Therefore, *we* also need to throw off the weights and the sin that so easily entangle us, and *we* need to run with perseverance the race marked out for us.

There is a race. There are goals to be accomplished. Whether we have discovered it or we are moving towards something. It may be hard to overcome *the weight* sometimes. It may be hard to get through *the sin* sometimes. We may need help, and we may need leverage, or a tool that can help us get through *that sin* and *that weight*. Opportunity Season has the potential to be a tool to give you leverages to move toward your desired life.

An interesting passage from Ecclesiastes (Chapter 4, verses 9 throuhg12) states that two are better than one because they have a good return for their work. Part of the logic, here, is that if one falls down, his friend can help him up. It also says, *"But pity the man who falls and has no one to help him up."* This is what can happen to us when we try self-help programs or self-help solutions. We do not have anyone to help us up when we fall; and, we inevitably fall. Many self-help programs suggest involving someone—your wife, your friend, or someone—to help you achieve your goals. This is great advice. Opportunity Season takes this one step further by presenting the formal concept of teammates and a team. When you fall down in this system, there is always someone else in place to pick you up.

The passage in Ecclesiastes continues talking about the danger of being overpowered. It states that two can defend themselves better than one. When things are coming against us, we are better off facing these problems with a partner. The last part of this passage says that a cord of three strands is not quickly broken. Accordingly, in an Opportunity Season, we invite the Lord to make a *three-stranded cord*, acknowledging that we are strengthened by a teammate, a team and the Lord. When pulling these principles together, a powerful tool is created.

One of the most important parts of the season is working with a teammate. A teammate can be just about anyone who is willing to work with you and listen to you as you both work on your opportunities together. You may want to work with a peer or a friend, but that is not necessary for an Opportunity Season to be successful. It is important to find at least one person to be your teammate, and hopefully others who will want to form a team. Your teammate does not need to have common goals or vision, but needs to be someone who cares about you as a person. It is also important that they are committed to complete the season.

You may be thinking that it will be hard enough to find one person, much less a team, to participate. How can people block out twelve weeks of time to participate fully? It is not as difficult as it may seem. It is OK to take time out from a season to go on vacation, play golf and goof off, just like you are living now. The important thing is to be in committed to completing the 12 weeks. I have been in seasons where work was going well and work was not going well. I have had parents die during a season. One of my teammates had a baby during a season. In good times and bad times stuff happens. Opportunity Season is just living life. Don't let the fact that you have some event or commitments coming up stop you from participating. You miss a game from time to time when you are on a baseball team; that doesn't mean you shouldn't participate or that you are kicked off the team. This is the same way. Participating in a season is much easier than you think.

One of the typical comments from previous participants is the camaraderie that develops between teammates. Many participants have never had someone, on a regular basis, communicate with them *specifically* about achieving **his goals *and* her dreams**, and vice versa. This camaraderie, in and of itself, is reason enough to participate in a season (and we're defining a season as 12 weeks). Your teammate should be someone who can keep your confidence and is willing to help you achieve your opportunities and goals. Hebrews 3:13 states that we should encourage one another daily. Opportunity Season takes this command seriously, and participants often experience the power of daily encouragement for the first time.

A good teammate will provide some of the attributes of a coach. Coaching is different than accountability or mentoring. I think accountability groups can be positive, and there is an accountability aspect that comes with being a good teammate. A coach will encourage as well as provide some discipline. Being honest with your teammate is critical. Let your yes be yes and your no be no. Telling the truth about a situation with compassion is many times what is needed. If you make a commitment to your teammate, it only follows that your teammate is going to hold you accountable for that.

Your teammate may or may not be your current friend. In friendships many times you will find that one of the persons will be enabling the other person to continue a bad behavior. What do I mean by this? I am not down on friendships–I think friendships are great! An example of how friends can enable your bad habits might look like this: something bad happens to you (let us say at work), and you feel you must talk to your friend about this bad thing that happened to you. Why is that? You feel bad and you want your friend to agree with you that the other person is wrong, reinforcing your right to be hurt. The other person who wronged you may be right or may be wrong, but you are seeking someone to agree with you.

The truth is that the person who made you upset might be correct in their comments. They could be wrong, or it might actually be the solution you need to move forward to solve a problem. A teammate is someone who is willing to explore the possibilities of the situation with you. A friend sometimes will not be willing to sacrifice the friendship to review the situation objectively. It is your season. You need to decide who will be the best teammate for you. Suffice it to say, it may or may not be a current friend.

A good teammate is probably not a family member. Family is great, and family is helpful; but, many times, family members have the same foibles and same problems that you do. It is great to go and talk with your Uncle Joe about problems, but many times Uncle Joe will give you answers that have already been resident in your family; or, again, will act in ways that will not challenge you because *you are family.*

What is the teammate dynamic? I am sure you have experienced it to some degree in other relationships. The relationship takes you to another level because there is commitment, discipline and accountability. There is also the aspect of encouragement and challenge. This encouragement and challenge gets ladled out at the discretion of the teammate; for your teammate does not want to exasperate you, but wants to push you to the highest level possible without having you get so frustrated that you quit. Why? Because your teammate cares about you and cares about the level of your performance.

This is where we started. A desire for a higher level of performance, a higher of level of success. You may have had relationships where someone took an interest in your success and made an impact on your life. It may have been many different types of situations: a Little League coach, a high school teacher, a manager, a mentor, a Sunday School teacher, or camp counselor. My experience has been that, unfortunately, these experiences of people impacting my life are too few and infrequent. Opportunity Season helps to institutionalize this experience so that you can participate in the power of community many times. You can participate in a season on a regular basis with different goals and opportunities being accomplished with each season. As you reflect on your life, have these type of relationships propelled you forward? If the answer is yes, then you know that it works. Why not do more of it?

Having a teammate can keep you from trying to *effort a goal*. What do I mean by "effort a goal"? It is very easy to think that if we just try harder at something, we will get more of it. Many times, when we try self-help programs, it is easy to not really change our behavior; we will just think we have changed. A teammate can see things that we do not see. They may see us spinning our wheels without making any progress. As individuals, we may not see any other solution to our problems except to keep trying what we have always tried and end up spinning in the same hole. Someone else can help push the car or suggest other solutions.

Teammates can also be examples to us in areas where they are strong. In Philippians 3:17, Paul says "join with others in following my examples, brother, and take note of those who live according to the pattern we gave you." When you have given permission to someone else to coach you, as a peer, it allows some powerful things to happen. Both of you bring a vast amount of experience to the table in the teammate situation. An even larger community is provided in the team situation, where you have six to eight people. A group of people who care about you are brought together with the intent of helping one another reach each other's goals. It is somewhat akin to the corporate power found in a board of directors of a corporation. If you desire a behavior to show up in your life, find someone with a passion for the behavior and learn from them why they are so excited about the activity. Most of the time, you will get excited also.

The name "Opportunity Season" deserves some discussion. Opportunity is used rather than goal to add a larger dimension to the three to five opportunities that a participant works on during a season. Opportunities are very similar to goals. A goal is something you want to achieve. It is measurable and should have a completion date. You have successfully met your goal if you hit your milestones and continue the course set before you. Setting goals is a powerful tool, and we will see that some of the opportunities in a season will be goals. However, the expansive definition of opportunities has to do with enlarging our vision, allowing for possibilities and the notion of working on spiritual results that may not be readily measurable. Some of your opportunities may explore possibilities and look for results that could be much larger than you think. Opportunities can expand your vision rather than limiting yourself to achieving a certain goal. God can show up and enlarge your vision in surprising ways.

Some of the opportunities will literally be a goal. (My goal is to weigh 175 pounds, my goal is to increase sales by 15% in the next 12 weeks, I will read one book per week for the entire season; these are goals.) However, an opportunity is also able to go beyond getting in shape or growing your business. For example, an opportunity may be improving my relationship with my daughter. Opportunities may also take on a spiritual dimension. God's calling on my life could easily be an opportunity; however, it is very hard to view this calling as a goal that I can measure in a specific time period. I can set up measurable tasks concerning my calling, such as reading a book about calling; but, I can also set the more expansive goal of praying about an opportunity, daily for a season, until I "hear" from God.

A season is 12 weeks, a calendar quarter. This is a typical length for a football or basketball season. A season is made up of games. Opportunity Season has 12 weekly games that make up a season. Each of these 12 weekly games is something that you try for a week. You may find it helpful, or you may find it just "so-so." That is OK, you're just playing a game—you are trying something for a week. Many of the weekly games will be a reason to move on and try something new. The weekly assignment may fall within your opportunity, meaning the specific opportunity you are trying to achieve for the entire 12 weeks, or it might end up being something you try for a week. Did it work? Yes or no, we won or we lost. Move on. You will get the idea as you participate. If you are a little confused, we will explain more of the rules in Chapter 2. It is your season and it is OK to add or change things that are unique to your team's season as you go.

What makes *Opportunity Season* different? Why isn't this book just another self-help book that promises to be the last self-help book you ever need? Opportunity Season draws on the knowledge you have acquired from all the opportunities you missed. Much of the information you will use in the season comes from all the self-help books that you purchased, all the seminars that you attended, or the sermons you have listened to. You attended a specific seminar or bought a specific book because it touched on an opportunity or an area in your life that you wanted to improve or perfect. Opportunity Season gives you a tool to implement and see results from all the stored knowledge you have acquired but not acted on. You know the things you want worked out in your life. You have an idea how to get there. Opportunity Season provides the tool, through the help of a teammate and team, and through the help of God, to accomplish the things in your heart. A *cord of three strands* to execute and turn into results all the good information you have acquired concerning opportunities that have excited you over the years. You probably already have all the knowledge that you need in a certain area. All you are lacking is execution: the application of a tool that can make the knowledge more effective. What *Opportunity Season* does is to capitalize on all the **good stuff** that you've heard or learned in sermons, books and seminars.

How many seminars have you attended where, at the conclusion, the presenter says, "On Monday morning what I want you to do are these three things." You nod your head, expecting to start on Monday morning. How many of those three things did you do for an extended period of time? Few to zero. When you hear a great sermon and the pastor says, "What I would like you to do is take a little time this afternoon–you'll have some time, it's Sunday afternoon–and jot down three or four areas in your own life that you want to work on that specifically relate to this sermon." We just don't do it. It is not the lack of knowledge, its lack of application. Therefore, Opportunity Season is a 12 week, palatable format, which is not too long to stifle commitment, but long enough to allow accomplishment. A season can also be a start. Nothing says that you can not participate in another season with the same opportunities. Do another Opportunity Season. Just like a football, baseball, or basketball season, there is always next season. You can have different seasons and different emphases and different opportunities. You can have one season per year, or you can participate in four seasons a year (not suggested, three at the most). What you will find is that you are compressing time and achieving things in a season that you have wanted to accomplish for years. I predict that you will gain more ground in achieving your life goals in 12 weeks with the leverage of a good tool, than you will in a year without the use of a tool like Opportunity Season.

If you want a result to show up in your life, add it to your next season. You can use as many seasons as needed. Try it. You will like it.

So this is my challenge–learn the toolbox presented in the next chapter. Learn how the season operates, and then move on into 12 weeks of Opportunity Season. See your opportunities come to life, in your life, with the help of God, concerning the things he has put on your heart. *Right now*, set the date to start your season. All seasons have a starting date. The date comes and goes whether you are a participant or not. When a sports season starts, you show up at the start date and participate almost regardless of what is currently happening in your life. There is always stuff happening.

Set the date. Write it down here. _____.

This is when your first Opportunity Season will start. You may only be able to find one more participant to be your teammate by the start. That is OK, start on time, and make it an opportunity to have a team for your second season.

# Why Opportunity Season

**Hebrews11**

[32]And what more shall I say? I do not have time to tell about Gideon, Barak, Samson, Jephthah, David, Samuel and the prophets, [33]who through faith conquered kingdoms, administered justice, and gained what was promised; who shut the mouths of lions, [34]quenched the fury of the flames, and escaped the edge of the sword; **whose weakness was turned to strength**; and who became powerful in battle and routed foreign armies.

**Hebrews 12**

[1]Therefore, since we are surrounded by such a great cloud of witnesses, let us **throw off everything that hinders** and the sin that so easily entangles, and let us **run** with perseverance **the race** marked out for us

**Ecclesiastes 4**

[9] Two are better than one, because they have a good return for their work:

[10] **If one falls down, his friend can help him up.**

**But pity the man who falls and has no one to help him up!**
[11] Also, if two lie down together, they will keep warm. But how can one keep warm alone?
[12] Though one may be overpowered, two can defend themselves.
**A cord of three strands is not quickly broken.**


## Philippians 3
[17]Join with others in following my example, brothers, and take note of those who live according to the pattern we gave you.


## James 1
[22]Do not merely listen to the word, and so deceive yourselves. *Do* what it says. [23]Anyone who listens to the word but does not do what it says is like a man who looks at his face in a mirror [24]and, after looking at himself, goes away and immediately forgets what he looks like. [25]But the man who looks intently into the perfect law that gives freedom, and continues to do this, **not forgetting what he has heard, but doing it—he will be blessed in what he does.**


## Hebrews 3
[13]But **encourage one another daily,** as long as it is called Today, so that none of you may be hardened by sin's deceitfulness.

The best thing to do is just start your season.

Make the first call.

You can work out the details as you progress in the season.

The hardest part seems to be starting. So Start.

# Chapter 2
# Preparing for an Opportunity Season

Hopefully you set a date to start your Opportunity Season. What follows is the strategy of an Opportunity Season.

Your first task is to set up your community. Ask someone to be your teammate or your peer participant. This person should be someone who is interested in pursuing opportunities and goals in his or her life. They might be a current friend or they might be an acquaintance; might be older, might be younger, but preferably someone with goals that he or she wants to accomplish in his or her life. This version of Opportunity Season is Christian-based and uses the Bible extensively. Your participants must at least be open to Biblical principles and willing to memorize scripture verses. Start thinking, start praying, and start asking to find someone to be your teammate.

When you have a teammate, the two of you can participate in an Opportunity Season without additional participants. It is more desirable to find a team, which would consist of multiple teammate groups (two, four, six, or eight total participants) that would make up your team or your community. The team goes through and completes a season together. Your team could be structured as a part of a Sunday School class; it might be people from work, or other acquaintances. It really does not matter if the participants are from the same location or not because most, if not all, of the contact can be done by phone. Your wife or husband probably would not make a good teammate; they have a different role.

# Daily Call

A season is made up of two major parts or structures in addition to individual opportunities and assignments. One is the 10 minute daily call between teammates and the other is the 45 minute weekly game plan call with the entire team. The 10 minute daily call is with your teammate only. This call is usually conducted by phone for 10 minutes or less. The structure of this call is free-form. The call is started and finished with what we call a *quiet mind*. This will be explained further in a Weekly Game Plan, but basically a quiet mind means you take a moment to clear your mind from all the clutter that has been going on prior to the call. It allows both of you to focus on the call and separate the activity you were participating in prior to call as distinct from the call. A quiet mind can also be accomplished by an opening prayer. Sometimes you will open with prayer and then other times not–teammates design their call.

An agreed upon start time is set by teammates when organizing the season. Morning, noon or night is not important, whatever the time is, it is important that both of you can make the call consistently. What you will talk about specifically are your opportunities and what has been happening with you and your opportunities. Questions need to be asked about season opportunities, such as: Did you exercise this morning? Did you talk to your wife? Did you do the assignment? Questions will also be asked about weekly assignments, such as: Did you work on your memory verse? Have you started this week's assignment? Did you understand this week's assignment? This accountability is only part of a successful daily call. The other part of a call is centered around sharing the victories and providing encouragement and suggestions on how to accomplish your teammate's specific opportunities. As the season progresses, instead of a teammate challenging you, you will find you are encouraging one another as results are accomplished.

When you are having a specific problem with one of your opportunities, the daily call provides an excellent forum to ask your teammate for insight into the problem. Usually the suggestions or answers will be presented the next day after you both have had time *to mull over* possible solutions. Questions may also be observations that you have had as a result of participating in opportunities. This allows for brainstorming with your teammate. Talking things out with someone who is familiar with your situation can be very valuable. Many times discussions lead to assignments. These can be designed as challenges that have specific milestones and outcomes. Sometimes, both participants will talk about their opportunities; however, if the ten minutes runs out before both have had a chance to share, say good-bye and leave the topic for the next day. You will be talking tomorrow, so there is no rush. ***Honor the ten minute time period***, even if the discussion is *getting good*. The temptation is to go longer. I encourage you not to go longer. Close the call, either in prayer or quiet mind, and go on with your day. Have your journal out for the call to record assignments from your teammate or anything that strikes you as significant during the call.

Many teammates call only during the week. They do not call on the weekend–that is up to you. You can call six or seven days per week if you choose no problem. Work it out with your teammate so you make the call at least five days per week depending on both of your schedules. That is the structure of the 10 minute call. Want to change something about the 10 minute call, no problem, it is your season. Make it work for you.

You might feel a little awkward about starting the calls. My advice is to just start making the daily call and it will naturally develop. If your are having problems getting going, start by asking questions concerning the three to five opportunities you are working on. Simply ask your teammate to describe why they chose the opportunities they did. A dialogue will start even if you do not know the person well. I have had seasons where I did not know my teammate before starting. I also have participated in seasons where I have known my teammate very well before starting. It works fine either way. Sometimes I end up sharing more and sometimes I seem to be the one receiving the most information. It does not really matter. A dynamic happens that I can not describe to you unless you do it.

## Weekly Game Call

The other basic structure of a Season is the weekly game plan call. The entire team of two, four, six, or eight participants has a 45 minute weekly call. Usually, this will be a telephone conference call. This can be accomplished either through a conferencing feature available on a business phone, or it can be accomplished using a bridge from a telephone service provider. A bridge may cost a nominal fee, so you may need to have dues to pay for it. It is simpler to do the weekly call by phone rather than trying to get together. An alternative, if you do not have the telephone availability, and are in a similar location, is to meet for breakfast once a week and do the 45 minute weekly game plan. Twelve weekly game plans are included in this book. Choose a team captain to facilitate the weekly team call.

The team captain starts by getting the team to have a quiet mind as described above in the 10 minute call. The same objective is in view: to move from the distractions of the day and focus on the weekly call. It may take the form of prayer and sometimes it will not, but take a minute or two to get quiet. Notice, I said a minute or two; it can be longer but do not be afraid of silence on the call.

The captain can open the floor for discussion from teammates concerning what has been happening during the week, usually sharing successes. After this brief discussion time, the captain will start a discussion of the weekly game plan from the book. You can read portions from the book aloud if you like. Open the floor for additional discussion about the weekly topic presented in the book. Sometimes the team captain will want to *go around the room*, calling out each individual's name on the phone so that everyone is participating. It is important for the captain to do this from time to time because, as in all groups, some people tend to talk more than others. Call each person by name and say, "What did you think about this, Ken?" "What did you think about this, John?" and so on. The last part of the weekly call presents the assignment for the following week and the memory verse for the week. It is critical that everyone at least try the assignment.

The assignment is designed to challenge each participant on the team to stretch to do things they may have not done before. It may be something that you have wanted to do but just have not taken the time to do. It is critical that everyone at least try the assignment. If someone needs to miss the weekly call, his or her teammate should give him or her the assignment and recap him or her on the call. Everyone will be reading the weekly game plan from the book, but it is very important for the community to participate in *every* weekly call. Teammates many times will discuss the weekly call during the 10 minute daily call. Teammates can help each other complete the assignments and the memory work. These two basic structures make up the community part of the season.

## Individual Opportunities

The other critical element and the most important part of *your* season are the three to five opportunities each participant will individually be working on. As you recall from the previous chapter, opportunities are similar to goals. One of the ways you can structure your opportunities is to have one opportunity each for your body, soul, and spirit. You might want to have an opportunity in each category. In the body category you might want to work out more, you may want to lose a certain amount of weight, you might want to eat better–there are lots of different opportunities that could relate to the body.

In the soul category, you might pursue something to do with your mind. You may want to add a time management tool, read more, or make more calls as a salesman, or do a name memory course–whatever you choose for an opportunity to expand your soul.

A spiritual opportunity could take many forms. You might want to find out what God's call on your life is, you might want to have a daily quiet time, you might want to work on your marriage. I am sure you have been challenged to develop many attributes into your spiritual life in sermons or books.

There are many excellent books on opportunities to pursue in the twelve weeks of a season. If you are looking for opportunities and some additional ideas, I would suggest you look on your book shelf to review the books you have purchased over the years. There must have been some reason why you purchased these books when you did. If the reason is still valid make the concept of the book one of your opportunities. A list of some suggested opportunities are provided at the end of the first Weekly Game Plan.

I would also like to emphasize that opportunities

do not have to be big and grandiose. They can be as simple as cleaning the garage over the 12 week season. It may take a few weeks or a few hours, daily, but the structure of a season will help you accomplish this task that has been *bugging you for years*. You may think this is a silly opportunity for ninety days, but it somehow has not been accomplished, even with the best intensions, for months. Clean up your office, read one book per week, play more golf; many leisure activities can be part of your season to add balance to your life and season. One of my teammates had a goal of climbing what we call "14'ers" here in Colorado—mountains over 14,000 feet above sea level. The opportunities you choose are up to you. Opportunities can be very simple, like drinking a gallon of water per day; or they can be very complex. The book you are reading was the result of an opportunity over two Opportunity Seasons.

Most of your opportunities should have milestones and deadlines. That is one of the reasons for using a twelve week season: you have a finite amount of time to complete three to five opportunities. Each season should have at least three opportunities and no more than five. Try to have some *open-endedness* to some opportunities. Do not be afraid to think, hope and believe big. God just might surprise you with something that **you have not because you ask not**. Why not ask just to see what God might do. Look for the possibilities for something really fantastic happening. It can easily be the best ninety days of your life. It is your season. It is your life. You get the results and the life you make. Make it a good one.

Everyone will need a Season Journal. This can be a simple spiral notebook, large or small. You can carry it with you or put it in a desk. A Season Journal allows you to record your opportunities and write down the assignments. You will be journaling some of the assignments, writing down your teammates' opportunities, and just journaling and keeping track of the thoughts and ideas that show up during your season. Get a notebook for an Opportunities Journal before you start.

## General Rules of Opportunity Season

Here are a few rules to get you started. You can also add your own rules as the season progresses. These rules should help you have a better season.

**Rule No. 1** You absolutely must honor confidentiality. This is on two levels: the individual call, where only the two teammates know; and the team call, with the whole group. You cannot share something on the team call that was stated on the daily call without the permission of your teammate to reveal a certain piece of information. You can share anything you want about yourself, but things said on a team call are not for anyone else's consumption, including spouses. If you have permission, that is okay, but do not share any information from Opportunity Season from either the daily call or the team call without permission.

**Rule No. 2** Honor time commitments–ten minutes on the daily call and forty-five minutes on the weekly team call. They can be shorter, but they cannot be longer. This helps to focus you. It keeps you on task, and you are honoring people's time.

**Rule No. 3** It is okay to miss a call, but it is not okay to miss a call without informing your teammate before you miss. If you are going to miss a call, or be late, let your teammate or someone on the team know. If you do not let people know, they will worry about you, and it is rude.

**Rule No. 4** No negative self talk or whining for 12 weeks. You will be amazed how often your chatterbox tells you that you can not do certain things. Your mind chatters away,

**You**: "I am going to work out."

**Chatterbox**: "No, you need your rest."

**You**: "I need to work out etc. etc. etc . . ."

You need to take control of your chatterbox. Without discipline your mind just goes off. Instead of making a decision, and being done with it, your internal chatterbox goes on and on telling you all the "good" reasons why you can't or why you shouldn't. Stop all that negative self talk and whining, which is also complaining, for ninety days. That is it, no negative self-talk—none, never, over, **DONE!**

**Rule No. 5** I would prefer a media blackout. You may need to have media news for your job, but some of you are addicted to news. Here is an example: this summer, in Colorado, we had the Hayman Fire outside of Denver. When you heard the first news about the fire, you heard most, if not all, of the news about the fire that there was for that day. If you listened to it eight more times, the exact same report was repeated throughout the day. You only need to hear it once, and if something really big happened during the day, someone else in your office or some other connection will tell you about it. The news mainly contains negative messages, and these stories just clutter your mind. You could also be addicted to the nightly news talk shows as well, so use your judgment. My suggestions are to read a book, listen to a book, or listen to music.

**Rule No. 6**. Do not hide things concerning your opportunities or make decisions concerning your opportunities on your own. When you are making a decision about changing a behavior, do not make it in a vacuum. You have a teammate, talk to them about it. Many times, when we are taking ground in an area, we have a tendency to hide things; or, we think they are stupid. It is better to receive the help your teammate or team can provide. You will not receive input if you do not ask. SO ASK. You do not need to talk to everyone about it; talk to your teammate about it. Do not hide things or make decisions on your own when it comes to your opportunities. Make decisions concerning your opportunities with the help of your teammate. Allow your teammate *to meddle* a little bit.

**Rule No 7** Make your work, work; and your play, play. The season is not meant to be a stoic exercise. This is not meant to be discipline. This is meant to be an opportunity. We do not want *to effort*. We do not want to just work harder or faster at something. We are looking for results. The tendency, as Americans, is to think about leisure as we work (Where am I going on vacation? What am I going to do? How can I do that?); then, when we are at play, or on vacation, we are thinking about work. (I wonder what has happened? What's going on back at the office? I wonder if they are talking to this client? I wonder if they ordered that material?) Focus on what you are doing when you are doing it. If you are working, work. If you are playing, allow yourself to relax and forget about work. Do not let these two intrude on each other. If we can maintain this perspective, then we will not continue to *effort*; we will be focused on results. It is important not to let other activities intrude on the thing we are focused on at the time. It is okay to take a vacation during a season. Just let your teammate know.

**Rule No. 8** Have a *possibility attitude* to try new things. Make this happen both with opportunities and with assignments. The assignments are given for you to try different things.

**Rule No. 9** The only way you can lose at your season is if your teammate quits; not if you quit. It is you that loses if your teammate quits. This is the nature of the commitment you have to your teammate. You can talk them into letting you *turn down the volume*. You can idle your way through to the end of the game. But it is your teammate who is keeping you in the season, along with yourself. The only way for you to lose the season is if your teammate quits.

**Rule No. 10** You have a lifetime of seasons ahead of you. What may happen, when momentum starts in your opportunities, is that you will discover that there are ten additional opportunities you would like to reach. Do not allow yourself to go off on *rabbit trails*. You can make a decision to drop an opportunity and pick another one up, but the three to five that you start with would be the best to complete during your season. Focus on completing them and remember the other great opportunities for another season.

**Rule No. 11** Pray for yourself and pray for your teammate. In the Lord's Prayer we are to pray for our needs for each day, "Give us this day our daily bread." Many times it is easy to forget to pray for ourselves and pray specifically for others. Pray specifically for your opportunities and specifically for the opportunities of you teammate.

**Rule No. 12** Have fun! This is an overriding criterion

And last but not least (this really is not a rule), remember: it is *your* season. You make the rules. This book is not always right, and your teammate and your team might not always be right, but that is okay. We are trying to produce results. It is your season, it is your opportunity. You make the opportunities happen. You can make your own rules in addition to these rules as your season progresses.

I have included a jargon page at the end of this chapter to jog your memory. It is a simple structure. Keep it simple.

# Pre Season

Use your Pre-Season to start some activities to improve your season. Start right now by doing one activity that answers this question: what is one activity that would move me forward in my current occupational goal or current daily activities goal? For example, ask yourself, "What activity can I start tomorrow that would bring results to my primary work goal?" This activity should be directed toward important people who have influence over this goal. It might be customers, clients, your spouse, your boss or other important people in your life. Start that measurable activity right now. Just start to do this important activity every day, starting now. Whatever you want to commit to, just do it every day. If you miss one day, start the next day fresh and treat the day before as a lost game and play to win *today*.

In addition, start, right now, by doing some activities that answer the opposite question of the first question: what is one time-waster that you could quit now, and that you know would not impact any of your relationships? For some of you it might be what we talked about earlier, a news blackout. It may be wasting time walking to the coffee pot and gossiping along the way. It might be TV for only one hour per day. I am not saying you can not watch TV or listen to the radio or whatever activity you like to do, but what is one thing that is a time waster that you will quit doing? Whatever that is, quit it right now. Remember, a time-wasting activity is not something that is recreational or something that provides rest, relaxation, or refreshing. These are quality activities. We are talking pure time-wasters

These two activities; an activity you will do more of (you could already be doing it, but you need to do more of it), and an activity that you will stop (something you are doing that is not with people who are important to you and does not move any of your goals forward); are like the exercises an athlete does to initiate pre-season training. Thus, like an athlete in training, we are getting our muscles ready.

The final pre-season activity is designed to start you thinking big-picture about yourself. The thirty-thousand-feet-above-the-earth-airplane-view of your vision and calling. What has God called you to do and to be? Think about Philippians 3:12. Paul is talking about pressing toward the goal, not that he has already obtained all this or has already been made perfect, but he presses on to take hold of that for which Jesus Christ took hold of him. Start thinking about your macro life goals. Why did God take hold of me? What is my legacy? How can I make a difference?

To stimulate your thinking, your first assignment is to write your own eulogy. Write your own eulogy on paper as if you are a speaker at your funeral. (Don't get morbid on me.) Talk about yourself in the third person. Speak as if you are someone else looking at your life and legacy.

For example: "This is my friend Ken. He was an enthusiastic person. He cared about his family and was excited about helping others reaching their goals. He was a member if this church for many years and he . . . etc., etc."

Don't worry about understanding everything about an Opportunity Season. It will become clear to you as you participate. Don't be afraid to be a team captain and organize a team. This book will make it easy to be the captain and organize a team. You can even read straight from the book on the Team Call; your team will not be upset. You will find that a 10 minute call per day is not a burden, and that the 45 minute team calls are fun. If you have team members with no apparent teammates, you can assign teammates. It is so critical to get started. You can always have another season to change things and make them better.

Many team participants find that effectiveness increases with additional seasons. You should still find that your first game is very effective; but, after you have learned how all the *parts move*, how you relate, and how you work during a season, you will find that your second and third seasons will be more productive than the first. Most people, if they do one season, do another and another. Change teammates and your team and start a new season after an off season. It becomes a way of life. It feels fantastic to be productive toward your own calling.

Do not worry if all this seems a little confusing. You will work it out in the first season. Do not read the weekly game plans until you have started your season. The power of Opportunity Season is not in the information presented in this book. The power is in participating in a season. Make sure you have a teammate to start on the date you have chosen. Start the daily call, start the pre-season, and get moving. Once you start your season, you will find the momentum building. As your season moves along, work out the details during the season.

Make sure you start your season on the date you set, even if your start is simply to make phone calls to find a teammate.

## Pre-Season Assignments

Increase the activity level of one activity that affects your daily work

Stop one activity that is a pure time waster

Write your own eulogy.

When you have your teammate and your team in place, have an organizational team meeting to schedule the times for your daily call and weekly team call. Appoint a team captain.

This can be done by telephone if you like. Read the Weekly Game Plan #1 after your organizational meeting. The assignments at the end of the section are to be done after the call during the next week.

Have a blessed season!

# Opportunity Season Jargon

**Opportunity Season**   Twelve week period of legacy assessment and achievement accomplished with the help of a team and teammate

**Teammate**   Participant with whom you have your daily 10 minute call

**Team**   2, 4, 6, or 8 participants who each have a teammate. The Team participates in weekly calls and weekly assignments

**Team Captain**   Person picked by the Team to facilitate the Team Call

**Team Talk**   Discussion questions for the end of the Team Call

**Weekly Game Plan**   Weekly reading from *Opportunity Season*; weekly assignments and Weekly Team Call

**Opportunity**   Similar to a goal and can be a goal, but allows for a greater stretch. The results may be greater than the participant is able to determine or imagine at the start of an opportunity season. Also allows for *goals* that are not measurable; such as, what is God's call on my life? Usually 3–5 opportunities per season.

**Assignments**   Weekly tasks that are part of the Weekly Game Plan, designed to experiment in potentially new areas.

**10 Minute Daily Call**   Daily call between teammates. Keep short and to point. Discussion concerning personal opportunities or weekly assignments

**Weekly Team Call**    45 minute weekly conference call to discuss the Weekly Game Plan

**Season Journal** Notebook to write down opportunities, assignments and other *good stuff* that happens in the season

## Preparing for an Opportunity Season

**James 4**
²You want something but don't get it. You kill and covet, but you cannot have what you quarrel and fight. **You do not have, because you do not ask God.**

**1 Chronicles 4**
⁹There was a man named Jabez who was more distinguished than any of his brothers. His mother named him Jabez because his birth had been so painful. ¹⁰He was the one who prayed to the God of Israel, "Oh, that you would **bless me** and extend my lands! Please be with me in all that I do, your hand be with me, and keep me from harm so that I will be free from pain." And God granted his request. (NLT)

**Philippians 3**
*Pressing on Toward the Goal*
¹²Not that I have already obtained all this, or have already been made perfect, but I press on to *take hold of that for which Christ Jesus took hold of me.*

# Weekly Game Plan #1
# Teaming Up

The daily call with your teammate is probably the most powerful element of Opportunity Season, and the community that evolves as you participate in the season is life-changing. Therefore, in an Opportunity Season, community functions on two levels (your teammate and your team) in order to provide the crucial insight that is available from the combined experiences of a teammate and a team.

The memory verse for this week is Ecclesiastes 4: 9 and 10. "Two are better than one because they have a good return for their work. If one falls down his friend can help him up. But pity the man who falls and has no one to help him up." *Pity* the man who falls and has no one to help him up. I believe that the concept of having a teammate is the difference that makes Opportunity Season something more than a self-help program. The main premise of the season is built around a team and teammate who care about the things you uniquely care about and who are committed to you and your success.

One of the comments from previous participants is how fulfilling and how enjoyable it is to have someone else care about their specific goals and the specific things that are important to them personally. People tend be focused on themselves, their own goals and their own things. They seem to have barely enough time to care about their own goals and forget about helping others reach goals. There does not seem to be time to reach out to others. However, it is in the reaching out that the dynamic of the season finds its effectiveness.

Just as your teammate is responsible for your success, *you* are responsible for your teammate's success. Generally we take responsibility for our own actions, and we should. Many of the results achieved in your opportunities will happen because of your own efforts, driven by your motivation and your desire to change. But the thing that makes a season so much different, and so much more powerful than a self-help program, is the requirement to have a teammate who can hold up "a mirror" to show us who we are and keep us honest.

Teammates can have a unique perspective on some of the issues concerning our goals and opportunities. It is helpful when teammates point observations out and give assignments specifically to each other regarding the participant's achievement of individual opportunities. Assignments should be designed to help your teammate determine strategies that enhance his or her understanding of his or her opportunities.

I had a teammate who pointed out to me that I would say, "I hope to do this, this weekend;" or, "I will try to do this." He would be challenging me by giving me an assignment to implement one aspect of one of my opportunities in a specific period of time; but, unconscientiously, I would make an excuse every time by using the word "try" rather than making a commitment to the assignment. I had no idea I was doing this until he called me on it. He would ask me, "What does try look like? What does hope look like? If you only try something what will the result be?" I had no idea that my entire vocabulary was centered on giving myself escape hatches. I would not have known this was "standard operating procedure" for me were it not for a teammate who heard and understood what I was doing to myself, and had the ability to point it out.

It is also critical that your teammate be a coach, and

that you be coachable. It is important for you to observe life and learn. If you are willing to look at the results of your thoughts, activities and results, you can learn from them. You can observe the results and outcomes of certain behaviors. If you are willing to see the results of certain actions you can allow those observations to teach or coach you into better behaviors to get better results.

An example of this would be perfecting the skill of shooting free throws in basketball. It seems obvious, but if the ball is short of the hoop, you need to shoot it harder; if the shot is too long, you need to let up a bit. Many times, life is the same way. When you look at a behavior you are trying to change or an opportunity in your season, it is helpful to look at the results of your efforts and adjust them. You need to change something about the way you are pursuing a goal if you want a different result. A teammate can help you see and evaluate what you may need to change to produce a different result. Many times this suggestion can take the form of an assignment. When you participate in an Opportunity Season, as stated before, you give your teammate the right to "meddle" in your life a little bit. Not many people have that right, and it is hard to find someone willing to do this for you. By letting someone else "read your mail" with your permission, you, by design, give them the ability to help you in areas you may be "blind" to.

One of the crucial mistakes people make when trying to change results is to keep trying the same things, or the same devices, or the same technologies, (we have many names for these things), to achieve the opportunities that they desire. Invariably, when you do the same thing, you achieve the same result.

As a simple example, I remember trying to add exercise to my life. My original opportunity was to workout *about* three times a week. I decided the workout could happen in the morning; although, it might also happen in the afternoon. If I had time in the morning, I would workout. If I had time in the afternoon, I would workout. After following this plan for a period of time, I realized that it was not working. You would be surprised how long I fooled myself with this little mind game. I needed to come up with a new solution. That new solution was to wake up at 5:30 AM, and go workout. Once I had that consistency, I was able to exercise on a regular basis. The new result was a workout at least three times per week.

How does the teammate come into this? It is as simple as the statement, "Well Ken, did you exercise three times this week?"

"Well, no I didn't. I was going to, I was trying to, and I had good intentions to."

His job, as teammate and coach is to say, "Observe life and learn. Look at the results that are showing up in your life. They are not consistent with the opportunity that you are trying to achieve. You need to try something different. If you were to try something different, what would that look like?"

For me, what that looked like was to schedule this everyday, at the same time, so it happened. Specifically the schedule was Monday through Friday, and taking the weekends off. If I had a breakfast meeting, I did not worry about it because I still would get in three workouts in the week.

The idea is that the teammate needs to be committed to encourage me, challenge me and sometimes "get in my face" like a coach, even if the "medicine" is sometimes difficult to take or give. A teammate can also use prizes or penalties to get my attention. An example might be, "If you do not work out 3 times this week, we are agreeing that you will make a fifty-dollar donation to a candidate representing the opposite political party to that which you normally support." If you do not like the penalty, then work out, and you will not need to send the money. You will quickly find out how motivated to the opportunity you are. If you still do not work out, maybe the next week the donation will be upped to one hundred dollars. Obviously, if you are still not working out with a substantial penalty, you need to change something. You need to look at yourself to decide if working out is really an opportunity that you care about. This is great information. The good news is that I was able to determine if working out was important or not. If it was not important enough for me to do, I could use my energy in another area that was important to me, rather than fooling myself into thinking I am achieving a make-believe goal.

A teammate can observe your results and coach you to a different solution. You may think something is happening; but, either it is happening, or it is not happening. They can hear what you are saying and see the results. How we describe something gives powerful clues as to how we really feel. A teammate can be very helpful in this processing.

One more important function that a teammate can play is the role of confidant. One of our rules is to help each other by talking about the decisions and commitments we are making concerning our opportunities. It is important to talk to your teammate about your hopes, your goals, your dreams, your opportunities, how big you can be; in a non-threatening environment, with someone who is committed to you, and committed to your success. I find it is very easy to harbor our fantasies or dreams. It sounds something like this in our mind, "Well, if I wanted to, I could be president of this company. If I wanted to, I could write a book. If I wanted to, I could be a tri-athlete."

We use these excuses and believe that the only reason that we are not successful, in some area of our life, is because we are choosing not to. We allow ourselves to continue our same behaviors by allowing this fantasy. We think that as long as we know we can be great, as long as we know we could achieve, then it is not that we are unsuccessful, it is just that we have not decided to achieve this goal yet. Guess what, one year later, five years, X years later, those fantasies do not show up as opportunity realities with results. Somehow, just having the knowledge of potential success makes us feel better.

Suppose you tell your teammate that you would like to run a triathlon. Your teammate replies, "That would be great. How would that look? How would that show up in your life?"

**You:** "Well, I guess I would have to run, I'd have to bike, and I'd have to swim."

**Teammate**: "What do you think you would need to do first?"

**You:** "Well, I really enjoy biking, so why don't I try that first."

**Teammate**: "Okay, why don't you do some research on triathlons, and see how people train for them. Maybe you should start asking around to see who you know that runs triathlons."

**You:** "Okay"

**Teammate**: "So, by next Wednesday, you will have found someone who runs triathlons, and investigate what the bike riding portion of the event entails. If you have time, try to find out the milestones necessary for training. Are we agreed on that?"

**You:** "Yes, agreed," you say with a lump in your throat.

Now, we have something measurable and tangible

to move the goal forward. We no longer are operating in: I want to be, I could be, I should be. No more fantasy. Either I will work toward the goal or decide not to do triathlons. Maybe I will discover that 10k's would be a way to start. If that is what I decide and I actually start training for, then running 10k's is a fantastic result that is better than fooling myself into thinking I am a tri-athlete if I would only choose to be one. Yea, right!

The conversation next Wednesday could sound like, "You know I investigated this, and I thought this was a goal of mine, and it really was not."

**Teammate**: "Great, that's wonderful. What have you decided to do with your workout goals?"

In one hypothetical week, you were able to identify a fantasy, giving you time to focus on the goals that are really important to you. I can not emphasize enough how important this aspect of being a teammate is. Just this one discovery about your life would make this Opportunity Season worthwhile.

A second topic for this week is our opportunities. If possible, make your opportunities measurable, specific, and with a defined completion time. One of the Pre Season assignments was to write a eulogy. This eulogy was you talking about your life. Hopefully, this exercise stimulated some ideas about the legacy you want to leave. Some opportunities should have been sparked that would move you toward your legacy. Also, remember our discussion about body, soul, and spirit opportunities as a starting point. Some examples of Body, Soul and Spirit Opportunities are listed at the end of this Weekly Game Plan.

After you have chosen three to five opportunities for your season, it is important to make *before season displays* and *before season data points* concerning your opportunities. When the season is complete you will compare your before displays and data to after displays and data. You will know exactly the progress you made. An example of a before display could be a picture of you standing, with only your shorts on, in all your glory. We tend to think of ourselves about ten to fifteen pounds lighter than the camera shows we are. We also think of ourselves as younger. To eliminate a possibility of not understanding where we really are, we want to take a before picture. Additional data would be measurements like what our cholesterol is, what our blood pressure is, what our weight is, what our body fat percentage is, and other important data.

Other before data could take the form of logs. These could be time logs or business related logs. Logs of everything that goes in your mouth for 3 days. Logs of spiritual activities. Be creative so you will have some type of benchmark for each opportunity. If an opportunity involves a better relationship with your spouse, ask yourself, "What is going on now?" If you log how many times and for how long you talked to your wife or children for three days, you will **know** the amount of time spent. You will no longer need to guess or allow yourself the fantasy of, "Oh, I guess about . . ." Do you say thank you? Do you let your spouse talk to you with out interruption, and how many times? As the saying goes, the better the data the better the output.

If becoming a better golfer happens to be an opportunity, what is happening with your golf game now? Are you serious, do you practice, do you need a lesson? Be honest with yourself and you will be surprised what you learn about yourself. Before displays or paragraphs will give you a sense of where you are right now in a measurable fashion. You will see and know what your progress is.

Be Creative with your before displays and have fun with them.

## Team Talk

Have you set up a time for your Daily 10 minute call?

Do you have any Opportunities in mind?

# Assignment Week # 1

1. Decide on three to five opportunities that will make up your season.

2. Inform your teammate what your opportunities are.

3. Write a paragraph on each opportunity as though it were completed. As an example, if weight loss is an opportunity, the paragraph will be something like this: I feel so much better now that I have lost twenty-five pounds. My body fat percentage is down also. I have more energy, my clothes are fitting better, and I feel great about myself, etc. Write one paragraph for each one of your opportunities.

4. Catalog or make displays of where your level of achievement is right now before you start working on your opportunities.

5. News blackout at least for this week. It is okay to hear the news once just do not listen all day and all night. Enjoy doing rather than watching.

6. Read Weekly Game Plan #2 before next week's Team
   Call. Do this week's assignments before next week's
   team call. Follow this reading and doing pattern for
   the next 11 weeks.

# Memory Verse Week #1
## Ecclesiastes 4: 9 and 10

## Teaming Up
### Ecclesiastes 4
⁹ Two are better than one, because they have a
good return for their work: ¹⁰ If one falls down,
his friend can help him up. But *pity* the man
who falls and has *no one to help him up!*

### Hebrews 3
¹²See to it, brothers, that none of you has a sinful, unbelieving heart that turns away from the
living God. ¹³But *encourage one another daily*,
as long as it is called Today, so that none of you
may be hardened by sin's deceitfulness.

### Colossians 3
¹⁶Let the word of Christ dwell in you richly as you *teach
and admonish one another* with all wisdom, and as you
sing psalms, hymns and spiritual songs with gratitude
in your hearts to God. ¹⁷And whatever you do, whether
in word or deed, do it all in the name of the Lord
Jesus, giving thanks to God the Father through him.

**James 5**

$^{16}$Therefore *confess your sins to each other* and pray for each other so that you may be healed. The prayer of a righteous man is powerful and effective.

**Proverbs 27**

$^6$*Faithful are the wounds of a friend,* but the kisses of an enemy are lavish and deceitful. (KJV)

# Sample Body, Soul and Spirit Opportunities

## Body

Read or re-read a book on exercise

Hire a trainer and work with them for twelve weeks

Take golf, dance, ski, scuba, fly fishing, sailing, etc. lessons

Talk to a nutritionist

Join a weight loss group

## Soul

Read 1 new book per week

Listen to books on tape while commuting

Write and mail one Thank You per day

Enroll in a class to further your career

Learn to use a computer program or piece of equipment

Make more calls, cold calls, appointments

Ask for one thing you want each day

Get a day timer and use it

Clear the clutter in your office, desk, garage etc.
Delegate one new task per week

## Spirit

Start a quiet time
Read one chapter of Proverbs each day
Improve relationships with wife, kids, employees, co-workers
Contact one person per week from
college or previous jobs and ask an open
ended question concerning their life.
Ask God daily what is your call on my life
Singles *may* want to find a mate and take steps to
meet new people
Prayer walk a certain area
Pray passages of Scripture out loud
Start or attend a class pertaining something you
have wanted to learn about
Start a ministry that you have been thinking about

Regardless of the opportunities you choose, make sure you approach the opportunity with new information or look for new ways to accomplish the opportunity in a different way than you have tried before. If you desire different results, you must approach an opportunity in a different way to achieve different results. Be creative, and have fun.

# Weekly Game Plan #2
## Developing a Quiet Mind

This week we will explore having a quiet mind. You might think that this happens easily, but it appears that this is not the case. To introduce this we will explore the performance zone, or *being in the zone*. People seem to perform best when they are not too excited or too calm. Something like Goldilocks, when the porridge was not too hot and not too cold.

This situation often presents itself in sports. A football team needs to get the "first hit" to relax and play well. The line is well prepared to start the game, but they are just too hot mentally. The quarterback in the early part of the game may "sky the ball," throwing the ball way over the receivers' head, because he is too jazzed. It is not that the quarterback does not have the ability to connect with the receiver, he is just not relaxed and "in the game" yet.

A similar thing can happen when a player is too lethargic. He is not in the performance zone or focused. People may say his head is "just not in the game." On the one hand, we have a quarterback who is so focused and engaged that he is over-shooting the mark; but, we can also imagine a player who is so cold that he is lethargic. This situation can happen coming off the bench. The coach calls your name to get into the game. When you get out on the field, you are just looking around, and almost do not know where you are, because you were not expecting to play. Here you are, in the game, expected to perform, and it takes a couple of plays, a couple snaps of the ball before you start to actually participate or move into a performance zone. Why do you think the other team will many times "test" the player who was just put into the game.

This can happen for all of us on Mondays. We seem slowed down, and we are trying to get going. At other times, when things are going so well, we just can not seem to keep focused and blurt out something inappropriate. Our mind is spinning so fast nothing is accomplished.

In the psychological realm, the extreme of this is called bi-polar, or the old term manic-depressive. In the manic state, people can not get anything done because they are too jazzed up or, in the depressive state, they are so depressed that they can not perform.

In normal life this can show up as a lack of focus. This is often demonstrated by day-dreaming. Our mind is capable of such great capacity that it is always thinking. It is going down "rabbit trails" to try to fill up space. It seems so effortless to daydream. When you are listening to a public speaker, or reading something, the information presented can send your mind off in a different direction.

A presenter uses Chicago as an example, and you find yourself thinking, "Wow, I was thinking about going to Chicago; that would be a great time. Chicago, the loop, yeah, the trains. I wonder why we don't have trains here in my city, seems like it worked for them, but boy those skyscrapers in Chicago . . ." Your mind has just run off in a totally different direction. We are mentally running to and fro. Events make us anxious or frustrated. Not to belabor this, but the mind will find ways to fill extra space.

One of the ways to prevent this is to go to a quiet mind. Interestingly, a quiet mind works both to slow down and speed up the mind. Quieting your mind will slow you down if you are too jazzed, or warm you up if your mind is unfocused.

Scripture has some interesting things to say about

a quiet mind. Good things happen with a quiet mind. In Psalms 46:10, it says, "Be **still** and know that I am God." In essence, the psalmist is saying, "Be quiet." Psalm 23 says, "He makes me to lie down in green pastures. He leads me beside the quiet waters." He **makes** me lie down. Another passage in II Corinthians, talks about "**Taking captive** every thought." Philippians 4 talks about "Be anxious about nothing." In Hebrews 4:11, we hear this advice, "Let us therefore **make every effort** to enter the rest, that no one will fall by following the example of disobedience."

The words used in these scriptures: *taking captive the thoughts*, *make every effort* and a command to *be still* are very active verbs. We need to make an effort to enter into rest. The command is to lie down in green pastures. It is an active exercise to get your mind to quiet. It seems like it should be a very simple exercise, but the idea of making your mind quiet is not accomplished automatically. Even if you understand the benefits of a quiet mind and try to work at it, it is something you need to be reminded of; for, it requires discipline to maintain a quiet mind.

It is important to be focused at the beginning of and at the end of each Daily Call. It is also important to be focused and aware at the start of every Team Call. To accomplish this each call is started with a pause or moment of quiet. One teammate will remind the other to start with a quiet mind. This means that for a brief space of time neither will be speaking and both will be letting all the activity that was happening before the call fall away. The previous activity will be stopped and your mind will be ready to be totally focused on the new input of the call. This quick stop of activity focuses your mind.

Whatever you were doing before you started, by going to a quiet mind, it calms you and gets you focused.

You are ready to be engaged in the call, rather than letting whatever was happening in your mind just keep going. It is the same way at the end of the call. When you are done with the call, you process those thoughts, stop, and have a quiet mind. The call is over and you are ready to return to your other activities.

Prayer before and after can also function to quiet the mind. Especially if it is reflective of the goodness of God. A mind-picture of this is in Psalms 133:1–2. It says, "Behold, how good and pleasant it is for brethren to dwell together in unity." (KJV) This is the set up. It goes on to say that this worship-filled fellowship is like the oil on Aaron's head that flowed down his head, and to his beard, and then to the hem of his garment. Knowing that this oil represents a Holy Spirit experience, I want you to imagine the anointing oil of the Lord being poured on your head, moving down your face, out to the end of your chin, down your body, and to the hem of your garment. You are being totally saturated in the presence of God.

Thoughts may come in your mind and you let them go. Quietness just comes over you. You are aware of the presence of God. You relax, and you are able to think clearly. You have brought God into the activity that is at hand.

To add this discipline to our lives we need to heed the command to be still. When starting to learn to have a quiet mind, it is important to monitor the number of times that you have a quiet mind or that you intentionally quiet your mind during the day. Some suggested times to go to a quiet mind would be in between activities. When you are leaving your house, going to work, getting into the car, before you leave the garage, quiet your mind. End one activity and start the next activity with a quiet mind. Arrive at work, get your computer up and running, quiet your mind. As you progress through the tasks in your schedule, and in-between tasks, take a minute to quiet your mind.

This does not take a lot of time. It can happen in seconds or maybe a minute or two. You move into a very relaxed state that I am calling a "quiet mind." As you do this, you are acknowledging the fact that you need a quiet mind. In this state, you can be still and know that God is in control. If you become stressed during the day, go to a quiet mind. Between tasks, just pause to complete one task and focus on the next.

Count the number of times each day that you quiet your mind. The discipline of counting the number of times is needed because the verses say we must take every thought captive, which means that we must make an effort to move into rest, knowing that God is active also, making us to lie down. You have to direct your mind to be quiet. Your mind is amazing. When you direct it this way, it naturally will become focused. All you need to do is make a tick in your day planner each time you move to a quiet mind or stop to bring God into a situation by thinking of him and his blessing on you.

Isaiah 30:15 says, "This is what the sovereign Lord the Holy One of Israel says, 'in repentance and rest is your salvation. In quietness and trust is your strength.'" So again, our strength is coming from quietness and trust. This is not any kind of transcendental meditation, or trying to put our mind to sleep. We are bringing our mind and thoughts quiet. This is meditation as it is in the Bible, rather than transcendental meditation that focuses on a mantra to trick your mind into being still.

We just want to bring our mind quiet. Stop to think about the Lord. Reflect on the oil of the spirit flowing down around you. Just stop your mind from whirring and move into quietness. The idea is that, while thoughts tend to come in and out of your mind, you are focusing your mind and saying, "Okay, I'm completed with this task and I'm moving onto another task."

I found something really interesting. I have been on church boards and I have been on other secular boards. Both would struggle with difficult issues and wrangle with it, back and forth. On the church board, many times, someone would say, let's pray about it. The act of praying about it brought a quiet mind to the people there. It brought a focus to the group and brought a unity to the group because of the quietness of our minds, bringing God into the situation we became still and knew that God was God, as the Psalm said. The secular boards did not enjoy the benefit of this skill.

This is what we are trying to do. On a regular basis, on a disciplined basis, get a quiet mind. Sixteen times a day may be the right number. This is once every hour, to maintain focus and to keep ourselves in the performance zone. Not too jazzed up, not too lethargic, but in the performance zone. You can use the technique of a quiet mind to either get yourself moving and warmed up; or, if needed, calm yourself down to where your performance is steady.

### Team Talk
How are your 10 minute daily calls going?
Hear from each participant.
Do you understand what a quiet mind is?

# Assignment Week#2

Start and end each call with a quiet mind.
Record the number of times per day you quiet
your mind. Sixteen times per day is the goal.

## Memory Verse Week #2
### Isaiah 30:15

# Developing a Quiet Mind

**Psalm 46**
[10] "Be still, and know that I am God;
I will be exalted among the nations,
I will be exalted in the earth."

**Psalm 23**
[2] He **makes** me lie down in green pastures,
he leads me beside quiet waters.

**Isaiah 30**
[15] This is what the Sovereign LORD , the Holy One of
Israel, says: "In repentance and rest is your salvation,
**in quietness and trust is your strength**,but
you would have none of it.

**2 Corinthians 10**
[5]We demolish arguments and every pretension that sets
itself up against the knowledge of God, and we **take captive** every thought to make it obedient to Christ.

## Philippians 4

[6]Do not be anxious about anything, but in everything, by prayer and petition, with thanksgiving, present your requests to God. [7]And the peace of God, which transcends all understanding, will guard your hearts and your minds in Christ Jesus.

[8]Finally, brothers, whatever is true, whatever is noble, whatever is right, whatever is pure, whatever is lovely, whatever is admirable—if anything is excellent or praiseworthy—think about such things.

## Hebrews 4

9 There remains, then, a Sabbath-rest for the people of God; [10]for anyone who enters God's rest also rests from his own work, just as God did from his. [11]Let us, therefore, **make every effort** to enter that rest, so that no one will fall by following their example of disobedience.

## 2 Corinthians 10

[4]The weapons we fight with are not the weapons of the world. On the contrary, they have divine power to demolish strongholds. [5]We demolish arguments and every pretension that sets itself up against the knowledge of God, and we **take captive** every thought to make it obedient to Christ. [6]And we will be ready to punish every act of disobedience, once your obedience is complete.

# Weekly Game Plan # 3
## Cultivating Awareness

Today we will discuss the practice or the ability to be aware in our daily life. It is amazing how many of us just wander through life. We are not aware of the people around us. We are not aware of the things happening around us. We are not engaged, or hearing the people who we come in contact with. We just seem to be going through life.

I find it interesting how much you can really learn if you are only willing to look. Many times this will mean looking people in the eye. It means observing everyone; **all** the people around you. I am talking about clerks in a store, restaurant workers, co-workers, your wife, your kids, and people that you meet. Literally becoming aware or awake to the things that are happening around you.

I do not know if this happens to you, but when I am introduced to someone and I put out my hand to shake, I look down at my hand, rather than at the person. Two minutes later, I have forgotten what their name is. If I look at them in the face, see them, and take the time to be aware, I start to meet them and at least have a chance of putting a name with a face. When I work at being conscious while being introduced to people, I am able to imprint and connect with that person through their eyes, instead of trying to connect with their hand. This seems simple, but I find I need to work at becoming more aware of the people around me.

Another aspect of being aware is keeping straight the many tasks that we have to do daily. Just keeping all the balls in the air can be very exhausting. It is very easy not to focus on some very important events that can be part of our opportunities. For example, you are working at the computer, and one of your children comes up and says, "Dad I'd like to talk to you about something." Our response is, "Yeah, that's fine, okay, what do you want?" What is happening during this encounter? We keep focused on what we are doing on the computer. The things that are concerning the child are just simply "Yeah, yeah, what were you saying? I didn't quite get that?" If we would be engaged, we would be able to hear what the child was saying and react to them.

This does not mean we have to stop what we are doing if that is the most important task. It is okay to say to the child, "I'm busy right now, can we talk later?" We need to make a conscious decision to be focused on the work at the computer or to focus on and talk to the child. What is not okay is to act like we are engaged in talking to the child when both we and the child know that we are aware to the computer and not aware to the child.

The weekly game plans and assignments build on each other to give you a better season. One of the ways or techniques we can use to move from the computer to talking with the child is to use the technique of a quiet mind. For example, the child approaches us while we are working on the computer, we decide to be engaged and be aware of the need presented by the child at that time. To move from being present to the computer and becoming present to the child, we simply take a moment to let our mind go quiet, and then focus on the child. One of the powerful things about learning the skill of quieting our minds is being able to be aware of what is going on around us.

One of the other problems with being aware is our lack of focus on a particular task. Many times we tend to think about work when at play and think about play when at work. We are tempted to worry about other aspects of our lives while working on other issues. It is better to decide about an issue and move on. Let me give you an example. You are at work with a pile of things to be done. Your mind keeps going to and thinking about whether or not you should go to your daughter's soccer game that evening. You think about what your daughter would say if you don't go. You do a little more work. You think about what your wife will say if you get home late. You do a little more work. You think about what your boss will say if you are late on this project. You do a little more work. You get the pattern. Wouldn't it be better to just decide whether you will attend your daughter's game and be done with it? Yes or No? What ever the answer is, decide. Believe it, and move on. Let your yes be yes and your no be no. **Decide and move on**. If you continue to "stew," stop the task you are working on. Make the calls or arrangements necessary to "put the game decision to rest" and go back to work focused on the task at hand.

Many Bible verses address this topic. Ephesians 5:15 says, "Be careful then how you live. Not as unwise, but wise. *Making the most of every opportunity*, because the days are evil. Therefore do not be foolish, but understand what the Lords will is." In other words, seize the opportunities that are presented to us. Matthew 6:34 says, "Do not worry about tomorrow, for tomorrow will worry about itself. Each day has enough trouble of its own." We want to be able to focus on the day at hand, and what is going on in that day. Finally, Colossians 4:5 says, "Behave yourselves wisely in your relations with those of the outside world. Making the very most of the time and seizing the opportunity."

When we talk about being aware, we are talking about literally seizing the opportunities of the day and being aware of what is going on around us. Being aware of the people that are around us daily. Work at understanding who these people are, and also learning who we are not connecting with. I think you will be surprised at the people who you are ignoring that you think you are connecting with.

One of the skills that we want to develop to help us be aware of people is to look them in the eye when we are talking to them. When you look at people in the eye as you talk to them, it shows them that you value them, that you are listening to them, and that you want to hear what they are saying. You communicate that you want to hear what they are saying, and that you are not engaged elsewhere or thinking about something else. You are listening to them. While it is easy to think about your next comment, it takes work to actively listen and be present with what the other person is saying.

If you are not looking at people when they talk to you, start doing it. If you are not accustomed to looking at people when you talk to them, you will be amazed at which people look at you and which people do not look at you when you are talking to them. The other thing you can become aware of is how easy it is to look at some people in the eye when you talk to them, and how hard it is to look at others. This will give you clues to your relationship with these people. You may also become aware of the people who value you and look at you when they speak to you. Have fun. Be Aware.

If you are having trouble with this exercise, I would suggest that you get together with a friend, spouse, child, someone who you can trust, and just talk with them while looking at each in the eyes for fifteen minutes or more. Remember that when you are doing this you are on the clock. What you will find is, eventually, after the cumbersome beginning, you will begin to learn the skill and overcome the anxiety that can come with looking other people in the eye. With very little practice this will become a natural skill.

## Team Talk

Each participant describes at least one of their opportunities for this season.

## Assignment Week #3

1. Be aware of your surroundings and be engaged in every activity. That is clerks, co-workers, family, friends, and every opportunity that presents itself. Also be awake to opportunities that God brings your way.

2. Look everyone in the eye when you are having a conversation with them. If you find this difficult we are suggesting that you devote at least a 15 minute period dedicated to talking to a friend and forcing yourself, if necessary at first, to look them in the eye the entire time. Just converse with them until it becomes comfortable. Do not look away for the entire 15 minutes.

# Memory Verse Week #3
## Ephesians 5:15, 16 and 17.

# Cultivating Awareness

**Matthew 6**

[34]Therefore do not worry about tomorrow, for tomorrow will worry about itself. Each day has enough trouble of its own.

**Ephesians 5**

[15]Be very careful, then, how you live—not as unwise but as wise, [16]**making the most of every opportunity**, because the days are evil. [17]Therefore do not be foolish, but understand what the Lord's will is.

**Psalm 90**

[12] Teach us to number our days aright, that we may gain a heart of wisdom.

**Colossians 4**

[5]Behave yourselves wisely [living prudently and with discretion] in your relations with those of the outside world (the non-Christians), **making the very most of the time and seizing (buying up) the opportunity.** (TAB)

# Weekly Game Plan #4
## Mastering the Simple

This is the start of the fourth week of Opportunity Season. The end of this week marks one third of this season completed.

This week ponders if you are gaining momentum, or if your season is flattening out; if you are still excited, or maybe losing interest.

We want to emphasize, in this call, the destructive nature of self-sabotaging behaviors. Many times, especially as we are trying to take new ground, negative self-talk starts to creep in our lives. We may also allow negative people to influence our lives and we may start agreeing with them about not achieving new goals or new things in our lives.

We will focus on some simple things in our daily lives to determine if this is happening in our season. One simple thing is arriving at meetings on time. This may or may not be a problem for you, but if it is, it will demonstrate how small things can cause us problems in a big way. If you desire to arrive at all meetings on time, you will need to plan to be there and ready at least five minutes early. If you plan to be at a meeting exactly on time, invariably, things happen and you are not there on time. By planning to be there five minutes early, you have allowed for time to set yourself up, be prepared, and be present when the meeting starts.

If you are late for a meeting, you lose focus. You arrive at a meeting late and you need to *get up to speed* to where everyone else is. Often, they will back track for you. You feel embarrassed. Just by being late, many negative things happen to influence the effectiveness of the meeting and your effectiveness in the meeting–just for being five minutes late.

Next topic. Are you are frustrated in achieving some of your opportunities? Most of the advances that we make (or the ground we take) in our life is the result of the hard times, not the easy times. Many of our successes come from overcoming the problems or challenges in our life. Things that seem like a failure to us at first are often a stepping stone to help us reach our goals. Ironically, the *good stuff* happens because of our willingness to accept the potential problems associated with reaching for a goal.

As strange as it may sound, we tend to give ourselves additional hurdles to overcome in Opportunity Season. This stretching for things that may be out of our reach has the effect of helping us move toward our goals at an accelerated rate. By setting high opportunities, we move ourselves toward the goals quicker, but we may not fully achieve our opportunities. That is okay. More specifically, our opportunities are vehicles that help us integrate desirable attitudes in our life. The ultimate goal is to become who God designed us to be; or, said another way, to take hold of that for which we were taken hold, as Paul says in Philippians 3:12.

The ultimate goal is to live a life consistent with who we believe ourselves to be in God *and* demonstrate with our actions the attitudes we have. Our opportunities and values should be consistent with our core beliefs. Our core beliefs should also be consistent with our other beliefs, so we are not double-minded or divided in our being. We are looking to achieve specific goals and results, but these goals should be vehicles to help us become more consistent with our core beliefs. In our achieving we need to demonstrate the beatitudes Jesus talked about in Matthew, chapter 5. Become more persistent. Become more devoted to our family. Be accepting of new ideas and technologies. By setting up specific goals in what may be simple areas, we give ourselves the opportunity to grow in the areas or the attitudes that we want to be or to become.

Another important benefit that comes from reaching for opportunities is that we may find out some of the things that we do not want to be. Usually, we find out what we do not want to be is late. We do not want to be crabby. We do not want to be wasteful. We do not want to be absent-minded. We do not want to blame others or not be present. As we reflect and talk a little bit about the first third of Opportunity Season, we would like to also look at things that we can do to accelerate our season in order to pick up momentum. Part of the season is to understand that some of the problems we are facing, or goals that we have not quite achieved, are actually developing or working in us the attitudes or the *who we want to be* attitudes that we want to achieve.

For some reason, people who do not want to grow and achieve also like to stop other people from growing. These people tend to be victims of events rather than using events to help them grow. Victims are people who do not turn lemons into lemonade. Strangely, they seem to like the lemons. These victims seem to enjoy nothing better than wasting your time with nothing but babble or whining. You do not need to listen to them just to be polite. They can stop your forward progress, and you can not help them. They need to help themselves.

It becomes your responsibility to stop victims from "pouring garbage" in your head. You do not need to be rude, but you need to stop them from polluting your space. This week, be aware of any victims that you allow to take your time and positive energy. This means that if someone comes in your office, or if someone is talking to you by the water cooler (whatever the situation), and starts whining and complaining, it is your task not to participate. You can't stop them from complaining to you, but you can stop yourself from complaining back to them. When you indulge and complain back, it takes you down. If someone starts "whining" to you, it is your responsibility to recognize it and politely end the conversation. You may want to set up a penalty to pay your teammate if you indulge the behavior. The use of a "fine" to help your partner achieve his or her opportunities. An alternative to paying a fine to your teammate is to set up penalties for non-performance.

Have a great week, and continue to persevere in the next eight weeks of the season. Have fun. Run the race that is set before you.

## Team Talk
Are you frustrated with some of your opportunities? Suggestions from the Team to move an opportunity forward.

## Weekly Game Plan #4
Be five minutes early for all your appointments
Do not let victims complain to you. Stop the conversation before it starts. Use a "fine" if necessary to stop this destructive habit.

# Memory Verse #4
## Hebrews 12:1

# Mastering the Simple

### Hebrews 12

¹Therefore, since we are surrounded by such a great cloud of witnesses, let us **throw off everything that hinders** and the sin that so easily entangles, and let us run with perseverance the race marked out for us.

### Philippians 3

¹²Not that I have already obtained all this, or have already been made perfect, but I press on to take hold of that for which Christ Jesus took hold of me. ¹³Brothers, I do not consider myself yet to have taken hold of it. But one thing I do: Forgetting what is behind and **straining toward what is ahead**, ¹⁴I press on toward the goal to win the prize for which God has called me heavenward in Christ Jesus.

### Matthew 5

*The Beatitudes*

¹Now when he saw the crowds, he went up on a mountainside and sat down. His disciples came to him, ²and he began to teach them saying:

³"Blessed are the poor in spirit, for theirs is the kingdom of heaven. ⁴Blessed are those who mourn, for they will be comforted. ⁵Blessed are the meek, for they will inherit the earth. ⁶Blessed are those who hunger and thirst for righteousness, for they will be filled. ⁷Blessed are the merciful, for they will be shown mercy. ⁸Blessed are the pure in heart, for they will see God. ⁹Blessed are the peacemakers, for they will be called sons of God.

[10]Blessed are those who are persecuted because of righteousness,
 for theirs is the kingdom of heaven.
[11]"Blessed are you when people insult you, perse-
cute you and falsely say all kinds of evil against you
because of me. [12]Rejoice and be glad, because great
is your reward in heaven, for in the same way they
persecuted the prophets who were before you.

# Weekly Game Plan #5
## Discovering the Source of Happiness

You may think that happiness is the cause of good things happening to you. If you have the right job, if you have the right kids, if your kids are doing well in school, if you are living in the right house, if you have the right friends, and things are going well, then you are happy. You may also think that you just have some bad days. You think you just "woke up on the wrong side of the bed," or that things just aren't breaking your way today.

I really believe that happiness is a choice. We choose each day whether to be happy or not. It's our *response* to things that happen to us that controls our attitude, not the things that are happening to us. What it takes is us being proactive in our responses, choosing to have a positive attitude and choosing to look for the possibilities.

If you do not think that you can choose to have happiness or a positive, expectant attitude; think about the choice of being angry. It is a choice. You can allow yourself the luxury of being upset. It has its benefits. People leave you alone. "Ken's grumpy today, don't get in his way." You also do not need to stretch for your opportunities. You have a built in excuse for why things just are not going well. The list goes on but you get my point. You choose, in your responses to life, whether to be happy or grumpy. My dirty little secret is that, from time to time, I just choose to be grumpy and "let off a little steam." I choose this very seldom, because it always has a penalty associated with it. Selah (think about that).

It is amazing how many good things naturally happen for us mentally if we praise God in all situations, believing that all things are working together for our good. It might seem rather strange to thank God for the things in our life that we perceive as bad, but that's really the attitude that we need to have. It is His promise that all things are working together for good for us if we're called according to His purpose. It is almost too simple. All that is needed from us is to have a thankful attitude for the daily things that we experience in life. This simple act of praise seems to release God's power to work in our lives.

Paul saw the same thing happening to him, as he writes in Romans 7:21:

> So I find this law at work, when I want to do good evil is right there with me. For in my inner being I delight in God's law, but I see another law at work in the members of my body waging war against the law of my mind and making me a prisoner of the law of sin at work within my members. What a wretched man I am. Who will rescue me from the body of this body of death? Thanks be to God through Jesus Christ our Lord. So then I myself of my mind am a slave to God's law but in the sinful nature a slave to the law of sin.

So, Paul recognized the fact that there was this battle going on within him. His solution was accepting Christ and having Christ come into his life. I think Christians have a real advantage here; for, with acceptance of Christ comes the notion or the understanding of a kingdom perspective. I think that this perspective is what we often need to be able to understand the things that happen to us on a day-to-day basis. It is not our responsibility to change everything that happens to us or to insulate ourselves from everything bad that might happen to us.

It is our responsibility to *choose* how we will respond, and act to move positively toward the Beatitudes, or the larger concepts that we would like to see working in our lives as disciples. Having a kingdom first attitude. Having an attitude that we are moving towards the things that God has put in our heart. And willing to make choices consistent with that.

What I mean by making choices is literally choosing to be positive and responsive and give praise in any given situation. To make decisions. To let our yes be yes and our no be no, as it says in Matthew 5:37, without making excuses for ourselves.

By making decisions concerning things that happen to us, the result is that we are in control of those situations by our response. We can not control many of the things that are happening around us. We can control our response to them. We control the situation rather than the situation controlling us. The "bad day" is not in control. We are. Our expectations that are not met are only that, expectations that are usually out of our control anyway. I cannot control how someone will treat me. I can control how I will respond to them. By controlling my response and not becoming emotional, I can also release creativity to resolve the problem.

This is what leaders do. Leaders look through situations and they change the view or the perspective. Some would say that this is changing the paradigm through which you are looking at something. You can manage situations. You can change outcomes. But, you can do these things only if you are in control by not letting the situation be in control. Praise helps us find positive outcomes and positive responses to many situations that come into our life everyday.

It is amazing to me how quickly a negative comment can literally just take control over us. We let the circumstances around us dictate how we will respond to situations in our day and ultimately what happens in our weeks, and months, and years.

It merely takes a simple comment by someone saying they did not like the way we handled a situation. Or they did not like how we were acting in a given situation. Instead of making a decision whether they are right or they are wrong in their observation and moving on, we will mull and "play the tape in our heads" and gossip and allow it to brew and fester in us.

So, the verse this week talks about making choices and choosing: "This day I call heaven and earth as witnesses against you that I have set before you life and death, blessing and curses. Now *choose life* so that you and your children may live and that you may love the Lord your God. Listen to His voice, hold fast to Him, for the Lord is your life, and He will give you many years in the land He swore to give to your fathers, Abraham Isaac and Jacob" (Deut. 30:19 and 20). The verses before this are interesting. They concern offering life and death and choosing life starting in verse 11.

Let me give you a quick example. I was at the airport, waiting for a late plane to arrive. I was getting upset and just fussing. In the middle of this I just decided to not worry about it and free my mind to do other things. It worked. All of a sudden I was "redeeming the time" and thinking about creative things. In truth, I was planning some of the concepts I would share in this book.

## Team Talk

What positive "surprise" has happened to you during this season?

## Assignment Week#5

In one of your relationships this week provide leadership. And I do not know how that will play out for you so look for it. It might be at home, it might be at work, but look for a situation where you can choose and lead into a correct direction rather than allowing circumstances to work on you. Proactively choose and lead to change a situation in a positive manner.

Make a shift in attitude in a situation where you are bored. Waiting in line. Stopped at a light. Make a choice to praise. Change your outlook

Use negative situations that happen to you this week to trigger a response of praise to God in all things.

## Memory Verse Week #5
### Deuteronomy 30: 19, 20

## Discovering the Source of Happiness

**Deuteronomy 30**
[19] This day I call heaven and earth as witnesses against

you that I have set before you life and death, blessings and curses. Now *choose life*, so that you and your children may live [20] and that you may love the LORD your God, listen to his voice, and hold fast to him. For the LORD is your life, and he will give you many years in the land he swore to give to your fathers, Abraham, Isaac and Jacob.

## Joshua 24

[15] But if serving the LORD seems undesirable to you, then *choose for yourselves* this day whom you will serve, whether the gods your forefathers served beyond the River, or the gods of the Amorites, in whose land you are living. But as for me and my household, we will serve the LORD."

## Romans 8

*More Than Conquerors*

[28] And we know that in **all things** God works for the good of those who love him, who have been called according to his purpose.

## 1 Thessalonians 5

[18] give thanks in **all circumstances,** for this is God's will for you in Christ Jesus.

# Weekly Game Plan #6
## Asking the Right Questions

Most of us would rather tell people what we know, rather than listen to what they know. We tend to be tellers of information, rather than questioners and listeners. People like to tell others about themselves, rather than listen to others tell about themselves or the information they possess.

The interesting thing about questions is that they control the dialogue. Questions are the rudder that directs conversation. The person who is asking quality questions is really the person who benefits most from a dialogue.

When a question is asked the mind is ready to answer. It is almost as if the mind can not stop from answering a question. You have probably noticed this phenomenon when asked by someone for information about a topic you do not want to discuss. When you are asked about something you are trying to hide you may say, "Oh, no I don't know anything about that." But you are betrayed by the look in your eye, or the way you carry yourself. They can see by your reaction that your mind answered the question, but you did not give up the answer. When asked a specific question, the mind's natural response is to want to answer that question. Sometimes this natural response can get you into trouble by betraying your real feelings. You may try to act calm when asked certain questions, but the quick response of your brain to answer the questions that are asked of you may tip the questioner that you know more than you are letting on.

The mind will answer questions when asked by someone else or by yourself. The mind will also continue to work on a question long after it is asked. I am sure you have had the experience of wondering about the answer to a question, when sometime later, "out of the blue," the answer is presented to you by your mind. It is a reflex of your mind. One of the minds "jobs" is to answer questions.

We can use this quality of our brains to help us solve problems and questions if we will only ask. Therefore one of the things we want to do during Opportunity Season is to ask ourselves quality questions. Many times if you can figure out what the question is, your mind will work on and find you the answer. To start your brain working for you in this way, all you needed to do is ask yourself open-ended questions about the opportunities of your season. Open-ended questions can have multiple answers. A closed-ended question is one that gives a yes or no answer, or just specific information. An example of a closed ended question would be, "Where do you live?" Answer: "Denver;" end of answer; end of brain process.

An example of an open-ended question would be, "What do you like about Denver?" The answer to this question opens your mind to an array of possible answers. You could answer by referencing the sunshine, the active life style, or your friends. The answers are unlimited, but they reflect your way of thinking.

What I am suggesting is different than "brainstorming," where you try to list any number of things that pop into your head. These questions, when addressed to yourself, will provide specific answers for you. If you ask the questions of others, the answer will be specific to and pertain to them. The critical thing is that you stop long enough to listen. You will be amazed about what you learn if you only listen to others and yourself.

It is critical when you ask yourself questions that

you allow your mind to ponder the answer. This is what I call *leaving the question open*. Sometimes, when you ask yourself a question, the mind will give you a quick answer. If you accept that answer, your mind quits pondering. If you take note of the answer, but leave the question open, your mind will continue to work on the question to come up with different answers. An unfortunate thing that can happen when you don't leave the question open is that you accept too small an answer or you only consider the obvious answers.

Examples of stopping your mind from pondering might be asking the question, "What would it take for me to witness to others about my faith?" Your mind may answer quickly, "You know you hate witnessing don't even think about it." If you accept this answer, your mind will end *the ponder* of the question and wait for the next instructions. If, on the other hand, you "listen to the answer," and leave the question open by thinking, "Maybe this is correct, but there must be some way I could witness;" then you allow your mind to continue to ponder the answer; and, potentially, at some unknown time in the future, your mind will present you with another option. If you like the option, you can choose to implement it; or, you can keep the question open.

Some examples of questions you might ask about your opportunities might be:

"Who do I know that understands exercise?"

"Who do I know that understands how to market my products?"

"Who do I know that can help me learn about non-profit organizations?"

"What is God's call for my life?"

"What is the most effective way to communicate with my children?"

By asking yourself quality questions, the solutions to many of your problems will be stimulated in your own mind. Many times, those answers will come instantaneously. They may also come when you "sleep on it."

My wife sometimes gets mad at me when we are trying to resolve a frustrating question and I say "Look, I just want to go to bed." This can be very frustrating for her because she does not want to go to bed; she wants to solve the problem right now, not later. But, my experience has been that with the way my mind works, I will often wake up with the answer. It can work the same when you ask your mind quality questions. Your mind will try to find the answer for you if you direct it correctly and truly are willing to "hear" the answer.

Another interesting aspect about asking others for answers to questions, or asking others for help, is that people generally want to help you. By asking the best people you know about certain issues, you will often get a quality answer. An example of a quality question when looking for information about doctors might be, "Do you know the best pediatrician in Denver?" By qualifying the question by using "best," "pediatrician," and "in Denver," you will potentially receive a much better response than to the question, "Do you know any doctors." The better question allows a specific response; but, more importantly, triggers the other person's brain to respond with the specific information you need. By directing this question more specifically, even to people in general, the question will flash responses in their mind directly to the question you asked. The better the question you ask, the better the answer you will receive.

Another thing that happens with questions is that they help other people decide for themselves. People like to persuade themselves about things. If you tell someone the solution to a problem, many times they will want to think about it or resist the solution. They often think that they need to provide an alternate solution. By starting a dialogue with someone and asking rather than telling, it gives the person the ability to do his or her own thinking. Your quality listening will also give you valuable information about his or her "take" on the problem. You can keep them talking with open ended comments such as: "Oh, that's an interesting point." Or, "I hadn't thought about that." Or, "Do you really think that?" Instead of rebutting their idea. Many times, people will continue to think and will come to a logical solution on their own. They will say things like, "Well, maybe it wasn't exactly that way." Or, "I guess I could look at it a little further." And by doing this, they end up talking themselves into your position, because many times they already understand the alternate position or alternate argument. If they do not understand the alternate argument, they will ask you a question and will be ready to listen to your point of view because you allowed them to think about it first.

You can start many different situations with a question rather than statement. If you are giving a presentation, the tone will be totally different if you prepare by asking yourself "What am I going to tell the participants?" or "What am I going to ask the participants?" This will totally change the tone of the meeting. Questions can be used in a myriad of ways. I want to give you two techniques that are similar, that play off this, and that will help you understand a couple of other ways you can use questions. When you meet a new fellow Christian, you might ask them a question similar to this: "What does being a Christian mean to you?" Usually, they will give you somewhat of a superficial answer at first. They will say something like, "It makes me feel so good." To which you need to reply with a follow up question similar to, "So, it makes you 'feel so good.' What does that mean?" To which they might pause and think and answer, "Well, it seems like I've got a lot more freedom from guilt." You can answer that question with another question (it must be asked with an attitude of wanting to listen to the answer). Something like, "So now that you're experiencing this freedom from guilt in Christ, how has that changed your life?" At that point, they probably will give you the right answer, or the reason why they either came to salvation or did not. You might end up with a diagnostic type question, which is used by a number of evangelism programs; such as, "If you were to die today and go to heaven, what answer would you give God to the question, 'Why should I let you into heaven?'"

The interesting thing that happens, when you use this technique correctly, is that, if you are willing to ask the follow up questions, there is a time when there is almost "a parting of the waters" that makes the two of you feel very connected. It feels as if the two of you are the only ones talking. You both feel it. There is a connection that happens when you are really communicating. This is very deep level of communication that can only be reached by asking open-ended questions. You must also ask the follow-up questions to "get to the connection point." As human beings, we seem to be programmed not to give our deep, true response too quickly.

People know when we are asking because we truly want to know. They need to know we care about them. It is critical that you are truly asking a question, and not probing for information. People will slowly give us more information if they are confident that we truly are seeking the information. Most people never learn other people's true feelings because they quit questioning and listening before they reach that connection point. It takes some practice to become a good questioner and listener.

My suggestion is that you try this with some of your friends until you can reach that connection point. You can use this technique with different areas of thought. You may choose money, since money touches so many things. Your lead question might be "Now that you have some money, what does having money really mean to you?" Or you might ask something concerning their position. "Now that you are on the church board, what does that mean to you?" Be creative. Try this a couple of times, and see what happens with it. The critical thing is to continue to ask questions until the connection happens. See if you can achieve that.

One last topic concerning questioning and listening. If you want to know how people feel rather than what they think, you need to ask how they feel about something, not what they think about something. Many take-charge personalities will only talk about what they think. I start by telling you what I think about a particular issue and you respond by telling me what you think about this issue. If we do not happen to agree on this issue quickly, we start a contest of, "This is what *I* think," to which they respond, "This is what *I* think," followed by, "This is what *I* think," and so on. Very little communication happens. You can change this dialogue by saying, "You know . . . I *feel* that you don't understand what I'm trying to say." Better yet, you might say, "I *feel* this is what you're trying to tell me." By moving from think to feel, from head to heart so to speak, you are saying "I'm not thinking about my response to you, I am telling you what I really feel." By using the words "I feel" rather than "I think," it triggers a different response.

I have used this with one of my daughters who seems to be much more of a "feel" type person rather than a "think" type person. Not that she does not think and think deeply. It seems that half of the world responds first as a thinker, and half of the world responds first as a feeler. It does not matter whether they are men or women.

I wanted to know how my daughter was planning her college schedule. My old way of confronting this issue would be to say, "I need to talk to you about something." This immediately communicated, "I'm going to tell you something," and her defenses went up. I decided to start by saying, "How do you feel about the way your schedule is coming together?" The first time I did this, I anticipated a strong response back, just the same as if I had said, "I need to talk (tell) to you about your college schedule." The absolute alternative thing happened. She ended up opening up and talking to me. It was very interesting for her to think that I actually wanted to know how she felt. She was already thinking about her schedule, and it was an emotional subject for her–she had feelings about it. So, when you move from thinking to feeling in your dialogue and in your questioning, it changes the whole dialogue and drops down the barriers.

You might say, "Well, if I would just tell her what she needs to know, I could convince her so that she would agree with me." What you are missing is that it does not matter what you know or what you can tell. You probably are right. But, if you do not connect with someone, and let them know how you feel, even if your solution is right, you will not even be able to communicate your solution. You need to gain my trust before I am willing to take the thoughts you have to heart.

This is especially true of people who are more feelers than thinkers. For many of you who are "tell-ers," you might want to try starting sentences or dialogues with the words "This is what I feel," rather than "This is what I think."

## Team Talk

1. Any question you would like to ask the team about one of your opportunities? They may be able to help you find solutions.
2. Are you a feeler or a thinker?

# Assignment Week #6

Ask God for something specific for yourself each day. Pray for your own success in the opportunities you are working on this season.

Try starting a dialogue with the words, "Here's how I feel;" not, "Here's what I think" about a particular topic.

Role play with your teammate on the daily call using the question, "What does your spiritual life mean to you?" Ask follow-up, "mirror "questions until you receive the "real" answer.

Try the role play with someone else concerning the question of what having money means, either to you, or with respect to your spiritual beliefs. Mirror-question until you connect with them.

# Memory verse Week #6
## I John 5:14–15

The verse talks about asking for things: "Ask and I will give." Compare this with these other Biblical phrases: "You have not because you ask not," and "If you lack wisdom, ask." God wants us to ask him.

# Asking the Right Questions

**1 John 5**
[14]This is the confidence we have in approaching God: that if we **ask anything** according to his will, he hears us. [15]And if we know that he hears us–whatever we ask–we know that we have what we asked of him.

**James 4**
[2]You want something but don't get it. You kill and covet, but you cannot have what you want. You quarrel and fight. **You do not have, because you do not ask** God.

**James 1**
[5]If any of you lacks wisdom, he should **ask** God, who gives generously to all without finding fault, and it will be given to him.

**John 16**
[24]Until now you have not asked for anything in my name. **Ask** and you will receive, and your joy will be complete.

**Matthew 21**
[22]If you believe, you will receive whatever you ask for in prayer."

# Weekly Game Plan #7
## Understanding Emotions

This week, we will discuss the relationship between our body, mind and emotions. I am using the example of emotions to help describe something that is deep inside of us that moves and motivates us. When trying to gain an understanding of how our body, mind and emotions interact, I have observed that the *methods of change* for the body can be easily understood; but, *the change itself* is slow to show up in our bodies. The mind or intellect takes a process to change usually started with a shift or a change in attitude that usually takes a period of time that begins with a paradigm shift. Finally, our emotions or feelings, which are deeper inside, are difficult to know how to change, but can change very quickly when ignited. I will leave it to the theologians to decide if we are designed by God to have a body, soul and spirit as talked about in I Thessalonians 5:23; or, simply a body and soul. For our purposes, we can gain understanding by talking about something we understand, emotions, even though this may reside in our soul rather than our spirit. We will discuss each part individually.

The methods for changing the body are well understood Most of us generally know what is needed to change our bodies. Usually, a change in diet and exercise is needed. Unfortunately, the process is slow. It does not happen in one night; it does not happen in one week, or even in one month. It happens over a period of time.

Our mind and thought processes seem to be shaped by habits. We do most things by habit because of the way we were taught, the things that we have learned, or simply the way that we do things. Habits are hard to break, and it usually takes a process to change, including a shift in thinking. Sometimes, just changing our thoughts in a given area can have amazing results. If you believe one way concerning an issue, and you change your thinking, this will often change your results or execution. This can happen with the coaching process. The coach says, "Why don't you try this? Why don't you look at it this way?" If we do, then it works, we retrain our patterns.

Advertisers or marketers use this process to understand what motivates us and what moves us. They use focus groups to find out the correct way to say something or the correct way to shape our thinking. However, it only motivates us and moves us if we are willing to shift our thinking. This process needs time to be worked out, because we have to learn how to think and react in different ways.

At times, our emotions can be the fastest thing to change. Emotions can act on us quickly. This makes changing our emotions difficult, because it is almost impossible to get a handle on them. An example of how quick your emotions can take charge is when you are deep in a thought. Your mind is fully engaged on a problem, and, "out of the blue," something happens and your emotions take charge. Your emotions just speed by your thought processes and you become wrapped up in the emotion. It can take less than a second for your emotions to run right around your thought process and take charge. An example would be you in your car, fully engaged in a teaching tape, when someone cuts you off. You know the rest of the story. The point is that you are along for the ride as long as your emotions are in charge.

Emotions can be both positive and negative. We can feel love, concern, or care. We can also feel anger or frustration. Negative or positive emotions can just come over us. However, if we control emotions before they start, we can often maintain control.

Earlier we tried to talk about the fact that one of the ways to make our mind more effective was to go to a quiet mind. Sometimes, if we just slow our mind down, we can gain control of it. It is important to develop the skill or the ability to gain control of your mind and not get needlessly drawn down a path of unproductive emotions.

I had a situation this week where I was trying to get a computer program to work. It should come as no surprise that someone with my skill level with computers was having problems. I had called my help desk, and they called the software vendor to solve my problem. All three of us were on the phone. I had bought the program with the suggestion of my help desk. They installed it. The confusion came about because the program I had purchased needed to be reinstalled. The manufacturer thought I had purchased the wrong program. They did not want to set me up with the correct program. The help desk knew the program I needed and had actually installed it on my computer previously. I am listening to these two computer techs discuss whether I would need to re-purchase the same program again. I was fine and merely listening to the discussion when all of a sudden, WHAM. My emotions took over. I was ready to let both of them know that I was tired of them wasting my time and potentially my money for a program I had already purchased. Fortunately, I had enough presence of mind to say, "Look, I'm getting off of this call. There's no point in me getting upset." And I hung up. They resolved the problem without me.

This detachment from a volatile situation was certainly easier because we were on the phone, and I could hang up. However, I have also trained myself by practice.

This does not mean that I am able to detach all the time, believe me. But, through prior self-training, I have begun to understand that, as emotions start to take over me, if I can stop, if I have an opportunity just before the flame is ignited and my emotions take control, if I can just stop and remove myself from the situation, then I can gain control. The emotions are still there, but I am less likely to blow up at people. If I am able to exit quickly, I only have to deal with my emotions. I do not need to deal with the fall out of bad behavior.

This is where I get the notion of the body being the gateway to the emotions. If we can train ourselves in low priority or practice situations we will be able to control ourselves when we are playing for real in the game. If we train on the small stuff, we will have the discipline when we come across difficult situations. This is what athletic teams do; they practice simulated game situations so that when they are playing the game, and it is on the line, they will perform the same as they did in practice. They should be able to do that, you would think if performance was only dependent on the mind understanding how to execute. If we understood what to do mentally, the result should just show up in the game. Wrong, because when you get in the game, the emotion of the game is there, and emotions are faster than your thoughts. However, by being able to slow down their emotions through practice, they are able to have a measure of control over their emotions. The discipline of the body gives them the insight into controlling their mind, which gives them the ability, in some cases, to control their emotions.

Another way this can show up is the notion or concept of praise. I was recently in a doctor's office. As you know, there is the public waiting room and then there is the real waiting room. The real waiting room is the little room where you sit in the room alone waiting for the doctor to enter. I was quickly brought from the large waiting room to the real waiting room. I brought a magazine with me and the nurse asked me some information, and then she left. After reading a few articles, the nurse reappeared and said that my test results were not back yet, so I would need to wait until the test results arrived.

Now, what I did next, I very seldom do; but, since I was in the middle of an Opportunity Season, I tried to operate in this principle. What I did was to praise God for the situation and changed my thinking. I would be in this waiting room whether I was fuming or calm. By changing my thinking from, "Where are the stupid test results? Why can't I talk to the doctor?" to, "I have some time while I'm here; I might as well make it productive and release creativity." This simple act of praising God allowed me to control the emotion of frustration just by being able to say, "Wait a second, I can take control of my mind; and, in this case, my emotions through my mind. I believe that by using praise in simple situations like this, I will be successful in harder situations by being able to control my emotions instead of taking the ride with my emotions.

Emotions are very fast. Because emotions can change so quickly, we need to train our responses. If we can only stop long enough to say a word of praise, or go to a quiet mind, our attitudes and emotions can help us, not hinder us. Positive emotions are where we get our passion. The interesting thing is how quickly our emotions can change when we change our thinking or change our patterns. If emotions do not take charge we can redirect. Praising God for all things is a great way to do this and learn to be thankful in *all* things.

## Team Talk
1. When have you experienced the "speed" of emotions?
2. How many times per day have you let you mind be quiet?

## Assignment Week #7:

1. Be aware of emotions and their speed. Be aware of the relationship between body, soul, and spirit.

2. Praise God and thank him for all things that come your way this week even if the situation is bad news.

## Memory Verse Week #7
## Hebrews 5:14

## Understanding Emotions

**Hebrews 5**

<sup>14</sup>But solid food is for the mature, who by **constant use have trained** themselves to distinguish good from evil.

**Hebrews 4**

<sup>12</sup>For the word of God is living and active. Sharper than any double-edged sword, it penetrates even to dividing soul and spirit, joints and marrow; it judges the thoughts and attitudes of the heart.

**1 Thessalonians 5**

[23]May God himself, the God of peace, sanctify you through and through. May your whole spirit, soul and body be kept blameless at the coming of our Lord Jesus Christ.

**1 Timothy 4**

[8]For physical training is of some value, but godliness has value for all things, holding promise for both the present life and the life to come.

**Philippians 3**

[19]Their destiny is destruction, their god is their stomach, and their glory is in their shame. Their mind is on earthly things.

**Ephesians 5**

[19]Speak to one another with psalms, hymns and spiritual songs. Sing and make music in your heart to the Lord, [20]always **giving thanks to God the Father for everything**, in the name of our Lord Jesus Christ.

**1 Thessalonians 5**

[18]**give thanks in all circumstances**, for this is God's will for you in Christ Jesus.

# Weekly Game Plan #8
## Dealing with Woundedness

This week we want to focus in on a specific emotion that may affect you. This emotion is the feeling of being wounded.

Frank Peretti, the Christian fictional author, has written a book called, *The Wounded Spirit*. In this book, he writes about the first time he revealed his wound or woundedness at a convention sponsored by Focus on the Family. He explained how an early childhood disease had caused him complications that caused him to lisp and stutter. He was also short in stature. While in junior high, he was bullied and teased because he was considered "weak." He felt very wounded. He goes on to present how he needed to be healed of that wound.

While he was speaking he thought that he had lost his audience. They were so quiet. Usually when he spoke, the audience was very responsive and having a good time. As he was sharing about his wound or woundedness, the audience went silent. What he discovered later was that he had touched a spot in people's lives that many times does not get touched. Specifically, the notion of an emotional wound, especially for men.

In another book, *Wild at Heart*, written by John Eldredge, this same topic of woundedness is addressed. Eldredge believes that every man needs the answer to the question, "Am I really a man?" He also maintains that boys are looking for their father, grandfather, or someone significant to them to answer and validate this question for them. Usually, the wound or validation comes from his father. Eldredge goes on to talk about how masculinity is bestowed from men to men. Only men can bestow manliness. It is something that is learned but not taught. It needs to be bestowed or validated by another male.

He believes that if men are wounded and do not receive healing for the wound it causes them to be posers or to have a false self. They often try to overcome their wound by over-compensating or becoming driven. This is sometimes demonstrated by very successful men who, while trying to prove their fathers wrong, can become workaholics. Another behavior that can manifest, according to Eldredge, is demonstrated by passive behaviors that suddenly become violent. It is difficult, and takes an effort, to deal with this wounded feeling. Eldredge's take on this, as well as mine, is that you need to work at finding a solution and also need a process to get your wounded heart back.

Part of the solution is an understanding of the quickness of emotions as discussed last week. They can almost instantly come over you. As men, we are very good at compartmentalizing our thoughts and emotions. We do not allow them to permeate our lives. Women tend to be much more holistic, if it is not working in one important area of their lives, it tends to color all other areas of their lives, and it is not working anywhere. Men, on the other hand, can compartmentalize. If it is not working at home, it can be okay at work. Men seem to be able to seal off other parts of their being and not address them. These emotions can seemingly lie dormant, but they really are festering under the surface. It seems easier to seal these emotions off rather than risk that, at some unexpected time, an emotion will flare up.

The emotion of woundedness can lie dormant only to "inexplicably" explode into full display. Many times the things that cause us to explode can be a clue as to where we feel wounded. The next time emotions explode, do not be afraid to ask yourself, "Why did that make me so angry?" and leave the question open, rather than just accepting the first thing that comes to your mind.

If you have a wound like this, it affects a large part of your entire personality, but you may want to deny it. From time to time it raises its head and you know it is there but you can never seem to get relief. The challenge I am making to you, is that you would have a willingness to explore your feelings and decide if you have been wounded.

I am not trying to play junior psychologist here. I am not trying to dredge up bad memories. But, I have seen the release and new power that can come to men who face and get healing from wounds given by their father or from other situations. The power seems to come from confessing the problem and forgiving the person who wounded you. Sometimes, a person will also need to forgive God for allowing this to happen. A person may also need to forgive themselves for "mistakes" they made that they *think* caused the problem or may have caused the problem.

Many times, as stated before, your father is the one you feel inflicted the pain. Some problem areas may be: forgiveness of your father for not allowing you to be yourself; not spending time with you because he was too busy at work; for not validating you because he was not emotionally sensitive. The hurt may come from many different areas, but if you feel wounded, you need to be willing to open up that "closed closet." With God's help, you will be able to find the hurt. It may be wise to pray with someone else concerning this and talk to a friend in a safe setting. It is important to *verbalize out loud* your forgiveness for your father, or whoever wounded you, for exactly what it was that caused the wound. O*ut loud,* you should specifically forgive them for the situation. Also, forgive yourself for holding that emotion and letting it have a measure of control over you.

The reason that I think this forgiveness is so powerful is that the Holy Spirit is the ultimate healer. As happens in salvation, old things can pass away and things become new. As part of working out our salvation, we need to deal with old wounds and allow cleansing to come in. It may happen quickly, or it may be a process; but, my point is that you may need to deal specifically with an area of woundedness.

Some people may want to go the person that wounded them and ask them for their forgiveness. This may or may not be a good idea. It is more important for you to get healed. The other person involved may not have any notion that they wounded you. I am not discouraging you from reaching out to the other party, but it is most important that you deal with your own issues.

I hope that I am communicating with you. Woundedness happens to many people. If you are not wounded, great. The reason that I bring this up in your Opportunity Season is that where you are wounded is many times where your true strength and genius will be. It is often from the areas where we are strong that our problems arise. For example, someone who is very outgoing and makes acquaintances very easily may offend their best friends by taking them for granted. A very honest person who is appreciated for their insights may offend other people because they are "so blunt" and hurt people's feelings. You know your own foibles. This may be why you feel so attacked in certain areas.

It is not uncommon that the things that people praise you for will be the same things they get upset with you about. If you are an enthusiastic person, people are encouraged by your enthusiasm and will praise you for it. At other times, they may criticize you and wonder why you are always kidding and joking around. They may even ponder why you have a problem being serious. So, the strength becomes the weakness. We need to be able to flow in the wholeness of our God given gifts.

This week's verse is Hebrews 4:12, "For the word of God is living and active, sharper than any double-edged sword. It penetrates even to the dividing soul and spirit, joints and marrow. It judges the thoughts and attitudes of the heart." My question is why do we need something to divide our soul and our spirit, our joints and our marrow? Why do we need to judge the thoughts and attitudes of our heart? My belief is that in this area of woundedness, because it is deep within us, even deeper than an emotional level, we need the help and understanding of the Holy Spirit to understand and deal with our wounds. Many times we also need to confess to other believers to obtain healing.

Another technique to deal with previous hurts is to write a letter to your father, or whoever wounded you, and explain the situation to him, forgive him, forgive yourself and then take the paper, crumple it up, burn it, throw it away, get rid of it, symbolizing the fact that it is gone. You are removing it from yourself. Journaling can help you develop your thoughts and get them fully out. When we write, we slow down our mind rather than operating at the speed of the emotion.

This week, ask God for understanding into your potential woundedness. Ask yourself, "Am I wounded and why?" Prayerfully explore this issue.

This is a hard topic. I know that. Take the time to make sure it gets dealt with correctly. If you need help or need to seek professional help, please do so. It is also important to understand that if you do not feel wounded, then you do not need to make-up a situation or try to make a situation in your life fit. It is important to open up the subject and deal with it if needed. It may be helpful to ask a trusted friend about situations you are not sure about. Again, if you discover the problem is greater than these simple exercises can solve, do not hesitate to seek out professional help.

## Team Talk
Do you understand the term wounded?
Can someone give an example of being wounded?

## Assignment Week #8

1. Talk with your teammate about this topic of woundedness. Tell them the story of when it happened if a situation comes to mind. Take the time to pray about and deal with it.

2. Write a letter you will not send to the offending party if you discover an area of woundedness. After completing it tear it up and dispose of it.

# Memory Verse #8
## Hebrews 4:12

# Dealing with Woundedness

**Hebrews 4**
[12]For the word of God is living and active. Sharper than any double-edged sword, it penetrates even to *dividing soul and spirit*, joints and marrow; it *judges the thoughts and attitudes of the heart.*

**James 5**
[16] Confess your faults one to another, and pray one for another, that ye may be healed. The effectual fervent prayer of a righteous man availeth much. (KJV)

**Psalm 139**
[23] *Search me*, O God, and *know my heart*; test me and know my anxious thoughts. [24] See if there is any offensive way in me, and lead me in the way everlasting.

# Weekly Game Plan #9
## Being Easy to Intreat

Are you easy to intreat? Are you willing to yield to reason? Are you considerate? James 3:17 talks about wisdom. The Amplified Bible version of this verse states that wisdom from above is first of all pure, then peace loving, courteous, considerate, and gentle. It is willing to yield to reason. Willing to yield to reason is translated "intreat" in the King James. The attributes of wisdom continue with: full of compassion and good fruits; it is wholehearted and straight forward; impartial and unfeigned; free from doubts, wavering and insincerity. Of these many great qualities listed, we will discuss the term, "intreat;" or, as defined by the Amplified Bible, "willing to yield to reason."

A friend of mine and sales trainer, Bob Dunwoody, was trying to discover and understand what successful sales people did differently than the rest of us. How did successful salespeople act differently? He was trying to determine this because he felt that he was not successful as a salesman. He felt if he could learn what successful salespeople did differently from himself he would be able to model them and become a successful salesman also. He started by identifying seventy successful salespeople. He called each on the phone and asked them if they would be willing to talk to him for a few minutes. To his surprise, all but one readily agreed to chat with him for a few minutes. He proceeded to question these successful salespeople, asking them what *they* thought made them successful.

Bob had his notepad ready to write down all the insights he was looking for. He discovered something different than he thought. These high producers had no idea that they were doing anything differently than the less successful salespeople around them. They just seemed to intuitively understand a way of doing things differently than the unsuccessful salespeople did. Bob thinks that about three percent of the population intuitively does things in a successful way and to them it seems natural. This makes it hard for them to explain why certain things make them successful.

One of the commonalities that Bob found in these successful salespeople was that they were always looking for the new and the best ways to do things. We might say they were easy to intreat. Conversely unsuccessful people like to "be right." For example, struggling salesmen will seem to know everything, and like to tell everyone else about the things they *know*.

I have known people, and I am sure you have known people, who **know** how everything should be. I had a friend who said the only TV to own was an RCA. Why? When he moved to Colorado, the only place to live in Colorado was Colorado Springs. Again, why? Some people I work with, who are not particularly successful, seem to always "know" the right way to do something and always resist any type of change. They do not like new computer programs; the old way is right. They do not want any change; the old way is right. If you have a question about anything, they are more than willing to tell you the problems with an organization, an idea, or a way of looking at things, because in their mind, they are "right." They are willing to fight to be "right." But, the thing about being "right" is that its only reward is that you are "right." The reward is that you are right, but only to yourself. Big deal. You might be right; you might be wrong. What matters are the results.

The way the world works is to pay for results. It does not reward effort or being right. The way that the system works is that results are the only thing that is rewarded and the only thing people care about. They only care if you are correct if it helps them to achieve higher results. It is important to remember that results, though desired, cannot be at any cost. You can over step your bounds. In a car deal that you worked too hard to "get the price," you may get the price, but lose relationship. In other words you "won" but really lost.

I have also observed that people who want to be "right" also want to win or care about basically insignificant things. This is a huge time waster for them. They spend hours defending insignificant positions. Plenty of banter about inconsequential things stated with great conviction. What I call "cocktail party chatter." Plenty of information, very little insight.

This phenomenon will also show up when winning small things, like maybe the football pool. On Monday, unsuccessful people spend a great deal of time telling everyone in the office that they won the football pool, how significant that was, and what a big deal that was. Now I have no problem with the football pool; I think that it is fun. But, I do not think that it is a wise use of your time or that you should try to gain significance from the fact that you won the football pool. It is somewhat of a random event, and if it is significant to you, and has meaning to you, that is great, and I hope you continue to win. But, if you just use this as a time-waster, and the twenty dollars you won cost you three or four hours of productive time, what is the point? (I understand that the football pool may be used as a team builder and may be useful as a conversation starter; but, are you operating out of this perspective?)

For Christians, I think this need to be "right" may take on a special distinction. We can easily have a problem with thinking we are right because, through the grace of God, we have learned many principles about life that are "correct." The Christian term for this is legalism. This is a problem for us, now; just as it was for the Pharisees in Jesus' day. People will split churches over "being right." Usually, the being right is concerning very, very small things. I fully understand there is a right-and-wrong, no question. But usually, the right-and-wrong people are worried about is not a Bible-based, defensible position. It is merely hearsay, and the position is not well thought out. Unfortunately, cliques can develop around these kinds of beliefs.

People will sometimes end up splitting up marriages concerning what is right about little things such as what to do at Christmas, or other holidays. The husband's family does it this way, the wife's family does it another way. What happened to the possibilities of getting together for Christmas to explore and enjoy family? They both want to be right and cause frustration and hardship for both sides.

There is a time to be right–to be correct about a topic. Some things are correct and are worth fighting for. Know what you know and speak with authority. Jesus was very easy to intreat. People loved him, he was very forgiving, he was not legalistic, and he did not have a problem being with tax collectors and sinners. But, he also amazed people by the way he spoke with authority. What I am trying to say here is do not be afraid to know what you know and speak it with authority. When you are being open-minded, and open to the possibilities, you do not need to give up your values. You do not need to compromise the things that you know that you know.

Successful people are generally lifetime learners; whereas, unsuccessful people "know" **everything** and like to waste time playing the game: *Know and Tell.* They know everything and like to tell everyone about it. People who are easy to intreat listen more than they tell because they are eager to learn new and better ways of doing things.

## Team Talk

Are you letting your team-mate "hold up the mirror" to you with a willingness to hear? Are you both encouraging and challenging your team-mate? Give an example.

## Assignment Week #9

1. Observe people around you to see if you can see this pattern of "being right" in people's lives. Do this to observe, not to judge. It is your choice then to deter-mine if you want to spend your time this way. Some-times you might want to.

2. Be aware of times this week when you need to be right or get into legalism rather than thinking about the possibilities.

# Memory Verse #9
## James 3:17

# Being Easy to Intreat

**James 3**

[16] For where envying and strife is, there is confusion and every evil work.[17] But the wisdom that is from above is first pure, then peaceable, gentle, and *easy to be intreated*, full of mercy and good fruits, without partiality, and without hypocrisy.[18] And the fruit of righteousness is sown in peace of them that make peace. (KJV)

**James 3**

[17]But the wisdom from above is first of all pure (undefiled); then it is peace-loving, courteous (considerate, gentle). [It is willing to] *yield to reason*, full of compassion and good fruits; it is wholehearted and straightforward, impartial and unfeigned (free from doubts, wavering, and insincerity). (TAB)

**2 Corinthians 3**

[17]Now the Lord is the Spirit, and where the Spirit of the Lord is, there is *freedom*.

**Galatians 5**

[1]It is for freedom that Christ has set us free. Stand firm, then, and do not let yourselves be burdened again by a yoke of slavery.

**Romans 10**

[3]Since they did not know the righteousness that comes from God and sought to establish their own, they did not submit to God's righteousness.

# Weekly Game Plan #10
## Seeking True Success

It seems that humans find it very easy to seek after things, to seek after stuff, to seek possessions, or to have things. Often, when we are looking at goals or looking at ways of improving we start looking at things. I want a new car, I want a new house, or I want more stuff. Even many goals-based programs will suggest that you should to take a picture of the Ferrari you want and tack it on your office wall so that you can imagine what you will have if you accomplish the goals you set out to do.

On the other hand, the Bible and Jesus talk about something very different. In Mathew 6: 33, Jesus tells us to seek first his kingdom and his righteousness and all these things will be given to us as well. The notion is that these things will be given to you later. Why is this so important? Proverbs 23:7 talks about the reality that, as a man thinks in his heart, so is he. And in James 4:2, it says you do not have because you do not ask God. But when you ask you do not receive because you ask with wrong motives that you may spend what you receive on your own pleasures.

Many times we believe that the getting things or having stuff is the first order of business. We start doing activities that will give us the things that we want. We mistakenly think that if we work hard to acquire the things we desire, we will be the person we want to be. We define ourselves by the big house we live in, the car we drive, or the stuff we own. We may even look to the skills we have to define our identity.

But, the Bible says that the most effective way to get the material possessions we need is to focus on who we are and what our heart is. Luke 6:45, states that the good man brings good things out of the good stored up in his heart. The evil man brings evil things out of the evil stored up in his heart. For out of the overflow of the heart the mouth speaks. If we listen to the things we say or blurt out to other people, we can discern the condition of our heart.

This concept goes way back. It was not invented in America. In Exodus 20:17, we hear instructions concerning coveting other peoples things. This instruction is part of the Ten Commandments, where the first thing talked about is our relationship to God, and then our relationship to others, including the kind of things that we do—such as coveting. We are not to covet other peoples' things or the things we do not have. We should not worry about the things we have or the things that we possess. "Covet" is one of those words that we do not use in our vocabulary very much, but coveting is forbidden. Therefore, coveting is something that we should not do. To covet is to desire what belongs to another.

What can happen to us when we covet first, instead first discovering who we are or what our heart is? What things should we seek first? When we covet, we may try too hard. We start to press people and get more interested in what happens to us rather than more interested in the people that are around us. When this happens, we totally move into a different space. In this state of being, only what I want is important; whatever happens to you does not matter. Winning matters too much. Therefore, a coveting attitude is set up around win - lose. I want your stuff and I don't care what happens to you. Rather than a win - win attitude.

It does not take us too long with this attitude, or in this space, to understand that it is not a long term proposition. We may obtain some short term results. These results come from pressing to obtain things and being motivated by stuff. But, the interesting thing is that the things we need will show up if we understand who we are and what our heart is. If we order things correctly, and first seek kingdom attitudes or *be* attitudes, both the material things we need and the correct attitudes we desire show up together. You get them both.

It is important to determine who we are first. Our goals and the things that we desire will naturally flow from who we are not what we want. Our values should determine our doings not our desires for material possessions. The results and things we need are initiated by first determining who God called us to be. The passions we have will provide the desire to work towards our goals. As we seek first the kingdom and seek who we are (what our vision is), things seem to naturally fall in line. Seek first God and his calling on your life and the things you should do and the things will show up naturally. Do not wish for things so you can be who you want to be. Instead, find out who you are and do things consistent with that, and you will have the things you want.

We are close to the end of this Opportunity Season. As you look at the opportunities you have chosen, determine if the things that you want to accomplish in your life flow from seeking the kingdom and your calling, rather than from coveting things your neighbor has.

This week's assignment is to review your opportunities and see if the results are motivated and in alignment with your core beliefs and attitudes. Determine if you have slipped into coveting or trying to seek stuff rather than the kingdom of God. Are your Opportunities consistent with your vision and the things that are really important to you?

Our Bible verse for this week is Proverbs 4:20–23: "My son, pay attention to what I say; listen closely to my word. Do not let them out of your sight, keep them within your heart; for they are life to those who find them and health to a man's whole body. **Above all else, guard your heart**, for it is the well-spring of life." It must be very easy to have our heart go astray if, above all else, it needs to be guarded.

Your heart, your vision, who you are, where you are going, what you are seeking first; that is the well spring of life. This is what will bring all things added to you; not coveting. Once you have found your heart and the Lord's calling on your life, be active in guarding your heart. Guard is an action verb. We need to be remembered by who we are rather than what we have. There is nothing wrong with stuff. We need stuff to further the kingdom, and we need resources to achieve our calling. The important question is, "What comes first, seeking or having?"

## Team Talk

Are you guarding your heart?
What does this mean?
Set a time for an after season celebration. Usually supper at a restaurant (more on this later, but set-up the time now).

## Assignment Week #10

1. Examine your opportunities to determine if you are seeking first the kingdom.

# Memory Verse Week #10
## Proverbs 4:20–23

# Seeking True Success

### Proverbs 4

20 My son, pay attention to what I say; listen closely to my words. 21 Do not let them out of your sight, keep them within your heart; 22 for they are *life to those who find them and health to a man's whole body*. 23 Above all else, *guard your heart, for it is the wellspring of life.*

### Proverbs 23

6Do not eat the bread of a miser; Nor desire his delicacies; 7For *as he thinks in his heart, so is he.*
"Eat and drink!" he says to you, But *his heart is not with you*. 8The morsel you have eaten, you will vomit up, And waste your pleasant words. (NKJV)

### Romans 1

20For since the creation of the world God's invisible qualities–his eternal power and divine nature–have been clearly seen, being understood from what has been made, so that men are without excuse. 21For although they knew God, they neither glorified him as God nor gave thanks to him, but their thinking became futile and their foolish hearts were darkened. 22*Although they claimed to be wise, they became fools*.

### James 4

1What causes fights and quarrels among you? Don't they come from your desires that battle within you? 2You want something but don't get it. You kill and covet, but you cannot have what you want. You quarrel and fight. *You do not have, because you do not ask God*. [3]When you ask, you do not receive, because you ask with wrong motives, that you may spend what you get on your pleasures.

## Luke 6

[44]Each tree is recognized by its own fruit. People do not pick figs from thornbushes, or grapes from briers. [45]The good man brings good things out of the *good stored up in his heart,* and the evil man brings evil things out of the evil stored up in his heart. For *out of the overflow of his heart his mouth speaks.*

## Matthew 6

[32]For the pagans run after all these things, and your heavenly Father knows that you need them. [33]*But seek first his kingdom and his righteousness, and all these things will be given to you as well.* [34]Therefore do not worry about tomorrow, for tomorrow will worry about itself. *Each day has enough trouble of its own.*

# Weekly Game Plan#11
## Stretching to New Heights

In Philippians 3:14, Paul talks about "pressing toward a goal, to win the prize for which God had called him heavenward." (KJV) In verse 15, he goes on to say that all of us who are mature should take such a view. He is talking about straining forward toward what is ahead, forgetting what was behind, and pressing towards this goal that God had called him to.

You have been involved in an Opportunity Season for a number of weeks now. Hopefully during that time you have been straining or pressing ahead toward the goal just like Paul talked about in Philippians 3. He forgot what was behind and moved towards what was ahead. He was engaged and moving forward.

Hebrews 5:14 also talks about us working toward and being engaged in the calling of God on our lives. "But solid food is for the mature who *because of practice* have their senses trained to discern good and evil." (NASB) *Because of practice* they have this discernment. *Because of practice* they are trained. Practice, or making a deliberate effort, is needed in our life to accomplish the calling of our individual Christian walk. We need to stretch and practice to move forward.

What I find interesting is that practice often causes or forces us to stretch and grow. Even more interesting is that when you are practicing and stretching to attain a higher level of accomplishment, the very act of stretching for the new level polishes or perfects the skills you are trying to develop at the first level of accomplishment. This is different than getting out of your comfort zone and trying something new. This polishing takes place almost automatically while you are trying to perfect the higher level skill.

Let me give you an example: I am from Colorado and I enjoy skiing with my family. If you know anything about skiing, you know the ski runs are coded by color. The beginner runs are color coded green; the intermediate runs are color coded blue; and the advanced runs are color coded black. As you are learning to ski, you start on the green runs. We will assume that you are past the "bunny hill," which would be for the "never ever" skiers. As you apply the things you have learned about skiing on the green runs, you soon find yourself very comfortable skiing on these runs. You feel great about your accomplishments. You like this. You like the fact that you can ski down this mountain and feel very comfortable while skiing.

It does not take too long before you want to "spread your wings." Confident with your new found skills, you decide to move to other parts of the mountain. You want to try some blue runs. What happens when you go on those blue, intermediate runs? Quickly, you are out of your comfort zone, you are stretching. You are using the same skills you were using on the green runs; except, half way down the blue run you realize that the speed at which you need to use your skills has increased. You wonder, "Why did I ever start going down these blue runs?" I was doing so well on the green runs. Now I am doing poorly and feel out of control. I will just go back to those green runs, and ski them until I get "advanced" at green runs. When I am *really, really* good at the green runs, then I will ski the blue runs.

There is a trap here. When you ski the more advanced blue runs, the mountain "teaches you to ski." The steepness of the mountain forces you to ski at a higher level. The skiing that you do on the green runs is automatically improved after you have struggled on the blue runs. By stretching yourself, you "automatically" improve how you ski on the green runs even though you think you may have become a worse skier while you were skiing on the blue runs.

What I am suggesting is that you have probably made substantial progress toward the opportunities in this season. You may be very comfortable with the accomplishments you have made. I know you have seen some great strides in your life. You might want to bask and feel comfortable at the levels you have reached. But, what I am suggesting to you is, if you are willing to stretch to the next level of achievement, then the act of stretching from the beginning area to the intermediate area, or moving from the intermediate to the advanced area will make you more accomplished at the goal. The stretching will enhance the skills you have acquired in the previous level. This phenomenon appears in many different places.

As you are trying to go to the higher level in skiing and other areas of life it is important to be in what I call the "ready position." In the "ready position," you have balance over your skis. You are ready to move in any direction you need to go; for, you do not know what the mountain is going to give you. In ballroom dancing you use the "ready position" because you can move forward or back or sideways depending on where your partner goes. The same thing happens with the linebacker in football. The defensive linemen in football have a primary responsibility to protect against a run. The defensive backs have a primary responsibility to protect against the pass. Therefore, the linebacker needs be able to defend the run or pass. The linebacker especially needs to be in the "ready position."

Many times, we need to be in the "ready position" as we are moving toward our goals and pressing to the next level. We need to adopt a ready position, because we are not quite comfortable with new things that may be happening to us. It is the same as when we were skiing the greens: we are very comfortable. We can handle the things that are coming our way. However, when we advance to ski the blue runs, we need to make sure that we are in the ready position. Our skiing improves because we need to negotiate what the mountain gives us. If we allow the mountain to "teach us," the experience of stretching will take us to the next level.

The Bible also talks about this, but I think it is in a little bit different way. The phrase "Fear not" is mentioned over 100 times in the Bible, usually to Bible characters where an angel is asking the believer to stretch, to move to the next level. You may ask, why did they say fear not? Well, there is a very simple answer. They were afraid. And it is the same thing that happens to us when we want to move from the greens to the blues. It is very logical that you would be afraid.

Hebrews contains another verse that touches this topic. Hebrews 11:7 says that "By faith, Noah, being warned of God of things not seen yet, *moved with fear*, prepared an ark to the saving of his house." You might think that Noah is moving with fear because he feared God. This is true. But, I think it is also referring to the fear Noah feels while he is out there building this ark. God told him to build an ark; so, he did just that. But, it is an emotional task as well as a physical task. Even with the fear he feels from friends, family and skeptics, he is doing the things necessary to complete the task. No one had even seen rain before. Noah is obeying, and he is taking his faith to the next level, even though he is moving with fear.

We need to move, even with our fears. We need to understand, "Fear not for I am with you, be not dismayed for I am thy God, I will strengthen you, I will help you, I will uphold you with my right hand" (Isaiah 41:10). If God is to accomplish the dreams that he has placed in us, then we will feel some fear as we move forward. We need the *fear not* verses because if we are taking new ground, having some fear goes with the territory. When we move forward, an interesting thing happens. As we move in fear to the next level, what was once fearful is now more comfortable. Just like in skiing. As we move on to the blue runs, the green runs we were originally fearful of are now very easy for us.

This week, think about where you can stretch forward concerning the opportunities you are working on. 1 Corinthians 9 talks about the fact that we have not seen, heard, or conceived what God had prepared for us. We need to stretch hard to begin to understand what God has for us.

With the final couple of weeks of this season I am making a mandatory assignment. It is critical to the success of your season that you complete this assignment. Coaches have practices and they sometimes have mandatory practices. This is a mandatory assignment or practice for your Opportunity Season. The assignment is described below.

## Team Talk

Do you have an example of a time you stretched to a new level and, after stretching, found you were more comfortable with the activity? Do you need to hear a "fear not" about one of your opportunities? Maybe you have already had a fear not in this season. Is the celebration banquet time set?

# Assignment Week #11

1. Write a paragraph about each opportunity that you have been working on this season. Specifically answer the question, "What would this area of my life be like if I was not participating in this Opportunity Season?" In each paragraph, you will discuss your before and after for each opportunity. Remember we started by reaching and stretching to see what could be accomplished in a twelve week season. Hopefully you have written some benchmarks from early in the season. This exercise will present us with the results of this Opportunity Season.

2. Be prepared to give each one on your team a copy of these paragraphs at the celebration banquet.

## Memory verse Week #11
### Hebrews 5: 13 and 14.

## Stretching to New Heights

**Hebrews 5**
[13] For everyone who partakes only of milk is not accustomed to the word of righteousness, for he is an infant.
[14] But solid food is for the mature, who *because of practice* have their senses trained to discern good and evil. (NASB)

**Philippians 3**
[13] Brethren, I do not regard myself as having laid hold of

it yet; but one thing I do: forgetting what lies behind and *reaching forward* to what lies ahead,
[14] I *press on toward the goal* for the prize of the upward call of God in Christ Jesus. [15] Let us therefore, as many as are perfect, have this attitude; and if in anything you have a different attitude, God will reveal that also to you: (NASB)

## Hebrews 11
[6]And without faith it is impossible to please God, because anyone who comes to him must believe that he exists and that he rewards those who earnestly seek him. [7]By faith Noah, when warned about things not yet seen, *in holy fear built an ark* to save his family. By his faith he condemned the world and became heir of the righteousness that comes by faith. [8]By faith Abraham, when called to go to a place he would later receive as his inheritance, obeyed and went, *even though he did not know where he was going*.

## Isaiah 41
[9] I took you from the ends of the earth, from its farthest corners I called you. I said, 'You are my servant'; I have chosen you and have not rejected you. [10] So *do not fear*, for I am with you; do not be dismayed, for I am your God. I will strengthen you and help you; I will uphold you with my righteous right hand. [11] "All who rage against you will surely be ashamed and disgraced; those who oppose you will be as nothing and perish.

## Proverbs 1
The *fear of the Lord is the beginning of knowledge*, but fools despise wisdom and discipline.

**1 Corinthians 2**

[9]However, as it is written: "No eye has seen, no ear has heard, no mind has conceived **what God has prepared for those who love him**"[10]but God has **revealed it to us** by his Spirit.

# Weekly Game Plan #12
## Becoming a Peculiar Person

Congratulations! You made it through the twelve weeks of an Opportunity Season. Hopefully you have seen progress toward your opportunities. Last week's exercise of writing a paragraph containing your before and after observations should have helped you discover how effective you were in accomplishing many aspects of your opportunities.

This last session is what I call the *peculiar advantage*. What I am labeling you today is peculiar. Only a peculiar people would have completed an Opportunity Season. This means that you are different from the crowd, that you are unusual, and that you are distinct.

When you look at the advances made in the industry that you work in, when you look at changes in the way that we approach things, or if you look at the changes that were made when Christ came to earth to confront a generation, they were accomplished and brought about by people whose ideas were considered to be a little strange when first introduced. The ideas seemed a little peculiar or maybe even a little bit deviant when people first heard them. I use that word "deviant" because of the descriptions in Hebrews 11:36 of heroes of the faith; some were jeered at, some were flogged, some were chained, some were put in prison, stoned, sawed in two, put to death by the sword, destitute, persecuted, and mistreated. While we do not want to be deviant in the sense that we are troublemakers, we may want to be a little bit of a troublemaker in the sense that we shake things up from time to time because we do some things differently than most people.

I am hoping you have become what I call a *one per-center*. This notion of the standard bell curve (the way that observations are distributed normally) was presented earlier. The majority of people, over 60%, are packed in the middle of the curve, just one standard deviation away from the mean or average. Almost 95% percent of the population is represented within two standard deviations away from the norm. If you move out into what are called the tails of the bell curve, or the 3% that is left, there are about 1 ½% that are far from the norm statistically, at the top end of the observations. It only follows that there are also 1 ½ % that are at the bottom range of the observations. This top 1 ½% is where the action is. These are the people that have an influence on the causes they are committed to and the things they are interested in. I am hoping that in the opportunities you have chosen that you are moving toward becoming this 1 % who have an influence on the things that are important to you.

If you are moving toward being a 1%'er, you are a peculiar person. According to Keller and Berry in the book, *The Influentials*, the decisions that influence where trends and thought are headed are made by only 10% of the population. The other 90% receive their information from the influential 10%. If you are a 1%'er, you go beyond this 10%, because you have **significant** influence on your world and the lives of those who come in contact with you. I believe that in the areas that you are focused on it will be people like you that make the breakthroughs.

It is interesting that the people who make break-throughs are willing to look at different ideas or different ways of doing things. An over-worked expression is that they are willing to "think outside the box." They are willing to look and think about things in a different way. Some of these ideas may sound a little bit crazy at the time, but these ideas sometimes work because people never thought about it that way, never learned it that way, or never tried it that way. When a new idea is put in place, sometimes and somehow, things *miraculously* change and there is a breakthrough.

I would also like to address the fact that the changes you are seeing or the strides you are making might seem small to you. It might seem to you that you could not affect the world by the opportunities or the goals that you have chosen. What I want you to understand is that the things that you do, the way you interact in your world and in your environment, is much the same as when you drop a rock into a pool. You may have dropped a boulder into a pool of water during your season, or your pool of influence. As the rippling effect moves out in rings from the ring started by you dropping the original rock, it produces an ever expanding ring or waves.

One of my fellow teammates went to a national conference of his co- workers, where people he had never met were coming up to him and talking about the changes they observed in his life. They had been affected and inspired by his successes. Many of these people were unknown to my friend before they came up to him. The ripples he was making in his season reached much further in his organization than he could have imagined or expected.

He found out that his actions could influence people from afar. He thought that maybe his word-of- mouth press releases were better than the reality. What I know about this person is that when others get to know him and understand him better they find out that he really is peculiar and special. My hope for you is that you are the type of person who as people learn more about you they decide that you truly are an exceptional person. My hope is that as people learn more about you they discover your genuineness rather than discovering that you are a phony. Unfortunately, this is not always the case. We all know of people or organizations that become less appealing as we learn more about them rather than more appealing.

As you think about and examine some of your relationships, I am sure there are people that as you get to know them better you like them more, eventually moving into loving them. Unfortunately, the opposite result can happen in other situations, as you learn more about some people you feel, "Wow, I thought this person was attractive," or, "I was attracted to him early on, but now as I find out more about him and his values, I realize that he is not attractive at all."

My hope for you is that, in your peculiar-ness, people get to know you and the reasons that you are peculiar; and that they will find you more attractive because of it. Hopefully, they will also be attracted to the things you are achieving.

Another unfortunate fact about some people who observe you taking ground in new areas is that some will want to *take you down*. I call those people crows. People who are sitting on the fence and watching you soar. They just caw, and talk at you as you soar higher. Do not worry about these people. Associate yourself with people that are moving on, people that are looking for change in their life, people who are like you because they are a little bit peculiar also. This final week, I want you to stop and relish, mull over, and even ruminate on how peculiar you felt for these last twelve weeks. Moving your life goals forward is exciting.

Your final assignment for this last week is to write a short paragraph, or bullet points, concerning what a magnificent next twelve months would look like in your life.

If your life was magnificent and fantastic, what would you be doing if you were living a magnificent life for the next year? This will give you a record to follow when you look back on the following twelve months. You can then do the exercise again for the next twelve months to build the life you were called to. You will have a record and be able to look at and really understand how magnificent and peculiar you are. I think you will find additional seasons will propel you toward your calling.

Our Bible verse for this week is 1 Peter 2: 9 and 10: "You are a chosen generation, a royal priesthood, a holy nation, a *peculiar* people. That you should show forth the praises of him that has *called you* out of darkness into his marvelous light." (KJV)

Thanks for taking the ride. Thanks for the journey. I hope you enjoyed it. Make sure you play another season and accomplish some of the additional opportunities that I am sure you became aware of as you were playing this season. Please e-mail me your results, victories and challenges at www.opportunityseason.com. Something quick and easy. Let me know you are out there.

## Team Talk
Any last thoughts and comments?

## Assignment Week #12

Write down your thoughts on the topic of A Magnificent Next 12 Months. Participate in the after season banquet and celebration with your team

# Memory Verse Week #12
## I Peter 2: 9 and 10

## Becoming a Peculiar Person

Peculiar - different from the usual or normal: curious odd; distinct

**1 Peter 2**
8 And a stone of stumbling, and a rock of offence, even to them which stumble at the word, being disobedient: whereunto also they were appointed.9 But ye are a chosen generation, a royal priesthood, an holy nation, a **peculiar people**; that ye should show forth the praises of him who hath called you out of darkness into his marvelous light;10 Which in time past were not a people, but are now the people of God: which had not obtained mercy, but now have obtained mercy. (KJV)

**Hebrews 11**
36Some faced jeers and flogging, while still others were chained and put in prison. 37They were stoned; they were sawed in two; they were put to death by the sword. They went about in sheepskins and goatskins, destitute, persecuted and mistreated–38**the world was not worthy of them**. They wandered in deserts and mountains, and in caves and holes in the ground. 39These were all commended for their faith, yet none of them received what had been promised. 40God had planned something better for us so that only together with us would they be made perfect.

## Mark 1

[3]"a voice of one calling in the desert, 'Prepare the way for the Lord, make straight paths for him.' [4]And so John came, baptizing in the desert region and preaching a baptism of repentance for the forgiveness of sins. [5]The whole Judean countryside and all the people of Jerusalem went out to him. Confessing their sins, they were baptized by him in the Jordan River. **[6]John wore clothing made of camel's hair, with a leather belt around his waist, and he ate locusts and wild honey.**

## 1 Peter 2

[10]Once you were not a people, but now you are the people of God; once you had not received mercy, but now you have received mercy. [11]Dear friends, I urge you, as *aliens and strangers in the world*, to abstain from sinful desires, which war against your soul.

# Chapter 3
## Off - Season

Congratulations! If you are reading this, you have successfully completed your first Opportunity Season. Congratulations are due because just completing an Opportunity Season is a great accomplishment. The fact that you both completed the course that was set before you is a great accomplishment.

Hopefully you completed your after season assignment of getting together for a victory banquet with your team. My guess is that you found it a very fulfilling time to get together face to face and talk with the people to whom you have been "baring your soul" on the phone. You are able see their reactions and share some of the successes and failures that you have had in Opportunity Season. I am also hoping that you have taken time to look at each one of your opportunities to see the progress you have made in your first Opportunity Season.

Upon completion of an Opportunity Season, most people have many emotions. Obviously, one of those is just being glad to be done, much the same as finishing a football season or a baseball season. It is something you can look back on with pride or look back with some regrets, wishing you had done some things differently. The good news is that there is always another season. There is always next season. This seems to be one of the most universal reactions to the end of the season. Glad that it is over, but also glad that the opportunity is to have another Opportunity Season.

I think one of the most powerful things that is built into Opportunity Season is the fact that it is a season. It lasts twelve weeks and then you get a chance to look back, reflect and try to understand what God was trying to teach you through the time that you spent using this tool for accelerated growth. I hope you were able to at least identify and slay a couple of chimeras in your own life. It is important to identify the things in our lives that are only an excuse not to put in the time to experience the real results that will add significance and success to our lives.

We discussed chimeras earlier and speculated that these make believe monsters are excuses used to kid yourself concerning the real you; potential barriers to your success that were only *wishes* and not *resolves* of the things you wanted in your life. Hopefully, Opportunity Season has enabled you to identify these chimeras, and even helped you to destroy some of them. It is not an easy thing to confront your own fears and foibles.

In the myth of the Chimera, the story has a happy ending. Bellapheron is the warrior that finally defeats the Chimera. He approaches the beast mounted on his steed, Pegasus (the flying horse), and is finally able to defeat the Chimera. It is a hard fought battle because the Chimera was a very fearsome, fire breathing foe. Bellapheron first tried to defeat him using his sword, stealth, and fighting abilities. When this failed he decided on a plan to use the beast's own power against him. In desperation, he took a block of lead and road his flying stead close to the Chimera, dropping the lead into its fiery mouth.

As the Chimera was using his fiery breath to attack Bellapheron, the intense heat was actually melting the lead. The lead went down the throat of the monster, suffocating him. This was the end of this incongruous, fire breathing monster that no one could defeat until Bellapheron came along. When he used the Chimera's own strength against itself, the very thing that made the Chimera seem so scary (the fire) was the force that destroyed the Chimera.

I am not smart enough to know exactly what the Greeks were trying to convey with this myth, but I do know that in my own life when, I have confronted Chimeras, I needed to confront the fictitious headlines I have made up for my life head on. It took the act of facing them and actually allowing them to dissipate of themselves to defeat them. The reason that Chimeras are self defeating is because they are not real. They are just things that we have made up and built up in our own minds to the point they are so real that they hold us back or fool us into thinking that we can or can not do certain things. The fact that they are not real makes them all the more difficult to remove from our lives. I am not trying to over work this myth, but I hope you have had some success with old foes in your life during Opportunity Season. If you have been able to destroy some of the illusions in your life, that are just fantasy, what a wonderful accomplishment. In my own life I have allowed some of my *myths* to have "power" over me for many years. Just exposing them to the light with your teammate and to yourself can show what a vapor they are. They can quickly disappear and the "strength" of them and the power that they seemed to have can quickly disappear under their own weight.

The other thing that I am hopeful that happened to you in your first Opportunity Season is that you started to understand what God's call or what God's purpose for your life is. I find it interesting, when talking to people who have completed an Opportunity Season that participants start to understand the things that are significant to them. They also start to understand some of the things that really are not as important as they thought. This usually develops a desire to participate in a second and additional seasons. I also find that when people do a second Opportunity Season, their opportunities become much more expansive and take on other dimensions that are not typically present in the first season (when they are starting to learn how to operate the tool). It takes some time to learn how help a teammate and learn from a teammate. You also need to learn how to function in the community of a team on a regular basis.

After people complete their first season–after a time of reflection and after a time of just relaxing–they are ready to participate in a second season. Usually, during this in-between time, they will find goals or opportunities that they will want to implement in their life. Sometimes, they will even try to implement them in their life and find out that they need the tool of an Opportunity Season to integrate them into their life.

As you start additional seasons (and I believe that you will), continue to pursue an understanding and defining of your calling. Pursue your significance and your legacy. Many of the opportunities worked on in a season lead to our own success in earning a living. This is a great use of Opportunity Season. An additional use for Opportunity Season is to add significance to your life, as suggested by Bob Buford in his great book, *Halftime*. Buford talks about the need for people to move on from success to significance with their lives.

Successes, as he is defining them, are all the things you obtain in life. The thrill of getting a career, not just a job; climbing the ladder and earning the money that you need to raise your family; providing a home for your wife and family; driving the car you have always wanted. You keep climbing Success Mountain until you get all the things that you need. I do not think this is a bad thing. I think these are all desirable things. God desires that we provide for our families. Opportunity Season can help you obtain the things that make you successful in life.

Buford presents the idea that, eventually, more success is not fulfilling any more. You can only have so much stuff. To find fulfillment in your life, he claims you need to move on towards what he calls significance. Success over the years is something that grows in your life and takes on dimension as you move from your twenties; where you will typically have a few of your goals in place (who you will marry, where you will live, and the career you will have); to your forties, when you see the fruition of many of your dreams. To see your kids grow up and see them move on. Hopefully, you will continue to enjoy the wife of your youth. There comes a time when success has overcome you and you realize that you really want something more. Your accomplishments are fulfilling, but somehow you still need something else.

For me, Opportunity Season was the thing that was able to break through and help me move into significance in my life. I was able to get rid of some chimeras that were clouding my calling and start directly working towards the things that were important to me. The things God had been working in my heart over the years. I have started to apprehend, with Paul, that for which I was apprehended.

To me, Opportunity Season finds its greatest power in helping you define, understand and start you moving toward your significance curve. Just like the success curve that started in your twenties, and comes to fruition sometime in your late thirties or early forties, you need to start a significance curve somewhere in your late thirties or early forties. Take the time to start growing and understanding your significance and calling. Take the time to define what is significant to you, what your calling is, and what God would have you give back. Because, just as the success was marked and defined by the many blessings and things that we get in life, significance ends up being demonstrated by the many things we give in life. The thing that God has put in your heart to give to your family, your community and the Christian Body.

Finding this drive, this passion, this call, is not an easy thing. My joy, happiness and significance came through finding a tool like Opportunity Season; which, through multiple seasons, started to bring significance to my life. I am hoping that through the Holy Spirit and the ability that he has given me, I have been able to communicate and transfer to you a few of these very simple concepts. It is my prayer that you will be blessed in multiple seasons, and that you will use this tool to develop the success curve of your life. I hope you will also define your significance curve and use this tool to implement strategies that will move your "giving back" forward also.

E- Mail me and let me know what happened. Also, look for *Opportunity Season: Next Season*, and the other materials that will be published. Thank you for helping me to be a success in this endeavor. I want to thank you for allowing me the great honor and privilege to work out my significance with God's help, by allowing me, through this book, to be a part of your success. Helping others launch their own dreams is my significance; my "one thing." If I reduce my significance to one word, the word is "launch." Through all my life, God has worked through and used me to help launch people into the things that God has called them to do. Opportunity Season has been a huge part of that vision and that significance for me. So, I want to thank you for taking the time to allow me to participate in my calling by your success.

Thank you for sharing this season with me and God bless your opportunities.

Find me at www.opportunityseason.com. I look forward to hearing from you.

# My Prayers for You

## 2 Thessalonians 1
[11]With this in mind, we constantly pray for you, that our God may count you worthy of his calling, and that *by his power he may fulfill every good purpose of yours* and every act prompted by your faith. [12]We pray this so that the name of our Lord Jesus may be glorified in you, and you in him, according to the grace of our God and the Lord Jesus Christ.

## Ecclesiastes 12
*Seek God in Early Life*
[1] Remember now your Creator in the days of your youth, Before the difficult days come, And the years draw near when you say, "I have no pleasure in them" (NKJV)

## Philippians 3
[11] If by any means I might attain unto the resurrection of the dead. [12] Not as though I had already attained, either were already perfect: but I follow after, if that I may *apprehend* that for which also I am *apprehended* of Christ Jesus. [13]Brethren, I count not myself to have apprehended: but this one thing I do, *forgetting those things which are behind, and reaching forth unto those things which are before.* (KJV)

# Opportunity Season Jargon

## Opportunity Season
Twelve week period of legacy assessment and achievement accomplished with the help of a team and teammate

## Teammate
Participant with whom you have your daily 10 minute call

## Team
2, 4, 6, or 8 participants who each have a teammate. The Team participates in weekly calls and weekly assignments

## Team Captain
Person picked by the Team to facilitate the Team Call

## Team Talk
Discussion questions for the end of the Team Call

## Weekly Game Plan
Weekly reading from *Opportunity Season*; weekly assignments and Weekly Team Call

## Opportunity
Similar to a goal and can be a goal, but allows for a greater stretch. The results may be greater than the participant is able to determine or imagine at the start of an opportunity season. Also allows for *goals* that are not measurable; such as, what is God's call on my life? Usually 3–5 opportunities per season.

## Assignments
Weekly tasks that are part of the Weekly Game Plan, designed to experiment in potentially new areas.

## 10 Minute Daily Call
Daily call between teammates. Keep short and to point. Discussion concerning personal opportunities or weekly assignments

## Weekly Team Call
45 minute weekly conference call to discuss the Weekly Game Plan

## Season Journal
Notebook to write down opportunities, assignments and other *good stuff* that happens in the season

TATE PUBLISHING & *Enterprises*

Tate Publishing is committed to excellence in the publishing industry. Our staff of highly trained professionals, including editors, graphic designers, and marketing personnel, work together to produce the very finest books available. The company reflects the philosophy established by the founders, based on Psalms 68:11,

"THE LORD GAVE THE WORD AND GREAT WAS THE COMPANY
OF THOSE WHO PUBLISHED IT."

If you would like further information, please call
1.888.361.9473
or visit our website
www.tatepublishing.com

TATE PUBLISHING & *Enterprises*, LLC
127 E. Trade Center Terrace
Mustang, Oklahoma 73064 USA